ACTIVE DIRECT...

NETWORK MANAGEMENT BEST PRACTICES FOR SYSTEM ADMINISTRATORS

4 BOOKS IN 1

BOOK 1
ACTIVE DIRECTORY ESSENTIALS: A BEGINNER'S GUIDE TO WINDOWS NETWORK MANAGEMENT

BOOK 2
MASTERING ACTIVE DIRECTORY: ADVANCED TECHNIQUES FOR SYSTEM ADMINISTRATORS

BOOK 3
SECURING ACTIVE DIRECTORY: STRATEGIES AND BEST PRACTICES FOR IT SECURITY PROFESSIONALS

BOOK 4
ACTIVE DIRECTORY TROUBLESHOOTING AND OPTIMIZATION: EXPERT TIPS FOR PEAK PERFORMANCE AND RESILIENCE

ROB BOTWRIGHT

Published by Rob Botwright
Library of Congress Cataloging-in-Publication Data
ISBN 978-1-83938-692-3
Cover design by Rizzo

Disclaimer

The contents of this book are based on extensive research and the best available historical sources. However, the author and publisher make no claims, promises, or guarantees about the accuracy, completeness, or adequacy of the information contained herein. The information in this book is provided on an "as is" basis, and the author and publisher disclaim any and all liability for any errors, omissions, or inaccuracies in the information or for any actions taken in reliance on such information. The opinions and views expressed in this book are those of the author and do not necessarily reflect the official policy or position of any organization or individual mentioned in this book. Any reference to specific people, places, or events is intended only to provide historical context and is not intended to defame or malign any group, individual, or entity. The information in this book is intended for educational and entertainment purposes only. It is not intended to be a substitute for professional advice or judgment. Readers are encouraged to conduct their own research and to seek professional advice where appropriate. Every effort has been made to obtain necessary permissions and acknowledgments for all images and other copyrighted material used in this book. Any errors or omissions in this regard are unintentional, and the author and publisher will correct them in future editions.

BOOK 1 - ACTIVE DIRECTORY ESSENTIALS: A BEGINNER'S GUIDE TO WINDOWS NETWORK MANAGEMENT

BOOK 2 - MASTERING ACTIVE DIRECTORY: ADVANCED TECHNIQUES FOR SYSTEM ADMINISTRATORS

BOOK 3 - SECURING ACTIVE DIRECTORY: STRATEGIES AND BEST PRACTICES FOR IT SECURITY PROFESSIONALS

BOOK 4 - ACTIVE DIRECTORY TROUBLESHOOTING AND OPTIMIZATION: EXPERT TIPS FOR PEAK PERFORMANCE AND RESILIENCE

Introduction

Welcome to the Active Directory Network Management Best Practices book bundle, designed to equip system administrators and IT security professionals with the knowledge and skills necessary to effectively manage, secure, troubleshoot, and optimize Active Directory environments.

Active Directory, Microsoft's directory service, lies at the heart of many organizations' IT infrastructures, serving as the centralized repository for user accounts, groups, computers, and other network resources. As such, it plays a critical role in enabling seamless authentication, authorization, and access control across enterprise networks.

This book bundle comprises four comprehensive guides, each focusing on different aspects of Active Directory management:

Book 1: "Active Directory Essentials: A Beginner's Guide to Windows Network Management" provides a solid foundation for those new to Active Directory. It covers the fundamental concepts, terminology, and basic operations necessary for managing a Windows-based network effectively.

Book 2: "Mastering Active Directory: Advanced Techniques for System Administrators" delves deeper into the intricacies of Active Directory management. From advanced group policy management to designing multi-domain architectures, this book equips experienced administrators with the skills needed to tackle complex network infrastructures.

Book 3: "Securing Active Directory: Strategies and Best Practices for IT Security Professionals" focuses on the critical task of securing Active Directory against various cyber threats. It covers authentication mechanisms, access control strategies, and audit policies to help IT security professionals safeguard their organization's network assets.

Book 4: "Active Directory Troubleshooting and Optimization: Expert Tips for Peak Performance and Resilience" addresses the challenges of diagnosing and resolving issues that may arise in Active Directory environments. With expert tips for optimization and resilience, this book empowers administrators to maintain peak performance and reliability.

Whether you're a beginner seeking to establish a solid understanding of Active Directory or an experienced professional looking to enhance your skills, this book bundle has something for everyone. By mastering the techniques outlined in these books, you'll be better equipped to manage, secure, troubleshoot, and optimize Active Directory environments, ensuring the smooth operation of your organization's network infrastructure.

BOOK 1
ACTIVE DIRECTORY ESSENTIALS
A BEGINNER'S GUIDE TO WINDOWS NETWORK
MANAGEMENT

ROB BOTWRIGHT

Chapter 1: Introduction to Active Directory

Active Directory, a pivotal component of Microsoft's Windows operating system environment, has a rich history and a significant evolution since its inception. Its development has been shaped by the growing needs of organizations for centralized network management, authentication, and access control. Understanding the historical context of Active Directory provides insight into its fundamental principles and its role in modern IT infrastructures.

Active Directory traces its roots back to the mid-1990s when Microsoft recognized the necessity for a centralized directory service to manage resources in enterprise networks. Prior to Active Directory, Windows environments relied on Windows NT Domain Services, which provided basic authentication and resource management capabilities but lacked scalability and flexibility for larger organizations. The introduction of Windows 2000 Server marked a significant milestone in Microsoft's network infrastructure offerings with the release of Active Directory.

Windows 2000 Server, released in February 2000, introduced Active Directory as a centralized directory service designed to facilitate the management of network resources such as users, computers, groups, and devices within a Windows domain. Active Directory represented a paradigm shift from the flat, decentralized model of Windows NT domains to a hierarchical, distributed directory structure based on the Lightweight Directory Access Protocol (LDAP) standard. This new architecture provided enhanced scalability, fault tolerance, and extensibility compared to its predecessor.

The core concepts of Active Directory include domains, forests, organizational units (OUs), and domain controllers. Domains serve as security boundaries within which users, groups, and computers are managed and authenticated. Multiple domains can be organized into a forest, which represents a collection of one or more domain trees sharing a common schema, configuration, and global catalog. Organizational units allow for logical grouping and delegation of administrative tasks within a domain.

The release of Windows Server 2003 in April 2003 brought significant improvements to Active Directory, including enhanced security features, increased scalability, and improved management tools. Windows Server 2003 introduced features such as the Active Directory Application Mode (ADAM), which provided lightweight directory services for applications requiring directory functionality without the overhead of a full domain controller.

With the release of Windows Server 2008 in February 2008, Active Directory underwent further enhancements to address the evolving needs of modern enterprises. Windows Server 2008 introduced features such as Read-Only Domain Controllers (RODCs), which improved security for branch office deployments by restricting access to sensitive information. Additionally, the introduction of the Active Directory Recycle Bin provided administrators with the ability to restore deleted objects more efficiently.

Windows Server 2012, released in September 2012, brought significant advancements to Active Directory, focusing on cloud integration, virtualization support, and enhanced management capabilities. Features such as Active Directory Dynamic Access Control (DAC) and Active Directory-based Activation (ADBA) further strengthened security and simplified management tasks. The introduction of the Active Directory Administrative Center (ADAC) provided a modern, web-based interface for managing Active Directory domains and objects.

Subsequent releases of Windows Server, including Windows Server 2016 and Windows Server 2019, continued to build upon the foundation laid by previous versions, with a focus on hybrid cloud integration, security enhancements, and scalability improvements. Features such as Azure Active Directory Connect and Active Directory Federation Services (AD FS) facilitate integration with cloud services and enable single sign-on (SSO) capabilities for hybrid environments.

Looking ahead, Active Directory remains a critical component of modern IT infrastructures, serving as the cornerstone of identity and access management for millions of organizations worldwide. As organizations continue to adopt cloud technologies and embrace hybrid environments, Active Directory will continue to evolve to meet the changing needs of the digital landscape. Whether deployed on-premises or in the cloud, Active Directory will remain integral to ensuring secure and efficient access to resources in enterprise networks.

In summary, the history and evolution of Active Directory reflect the ongoing efforts of Microsoft to provide organizations with a robust, scalable, and secure directory service solution. From its inception in Windows 2000 Server to its current role in hybrid cloud environments, Active Directory has continuously evolved to meet the challenges of modern IT infrastructures, making it a cornerstone of network management and identity and access management for organizations worldwide.

Active Directory, the centralized directory service developed by Microsoft, forms the backbone of authentication, authorization, and resource management in Windows-based environments. Understanding its core components and concepts is essential for effectively deploying, managing, and troubleshooting Active Directory environments.

Domains and Domain Controllers:

Domains are the foundational units of Active Directory, representing security boundaries within which users, groups, computers, and other objects are managed and authenticated. Each domain is administered by one or more domain controllers, which are Windows servers responsible for storing and replicating directory data, authenticating users, and enforcing security policies within the domain.

To deploy a domain controller using the command-line interface (CLI), administrators can use the **dcpromo** command on Windows Server:

bashCopy code

```
dcpromo /unattend
```

This command initiates an unattended installation of a domain controller, allowing administrators to automate the deployment process.

Forests and Trees:

A forest is a collection of one or more domains that share a common schema, configuration, and global catalog. Domains within a forest form a hierarchical structure known as a tree, with a single root domain at the top of the hierarchy. Trust relationships between domains enable users and resources to be shared securely across the forest.

To create a new forest using CLI commands, administrators can use the **New-ADForest** cmdlet in PowerShell:

sqlCopy code

```
New-ADForest -DomainName "example.com" -DomainMode "Windows2016Forest" -ForestMode "Windows2016Forest"
```

This command creates a new Active Directory forest named "example.com" with the specified domain and forest functional levels.

Organizational Units (OUs):

Organizational Units (OUs) provide a means of organizing and delegating administrative authority within a domain. OUs are containers that can hold users, groups, computers, and other objects, allowing administrators to apply Group Policy settings, permissions, and other configurations at a granular level.

To create a new organizational unit using CLI commands, administrators can use the **New-ADOrganizationalUnit** cmdlet in PowerShell:

mathematicaCopy code

```
New-ADOrganizationalUnit    -Name    "Sales"    -Path
"OU=Departments,DC=example,DC=com"
```

This command creates a new OU named "Sales" within the "Departments" OU in the "example.com" domain.

Group Policy Objects (GPOs):

Group Policy Objects (GPOs) are collections of settings that define how computers and users behave in an Active Directory environment. GPOs can be linked to sites, domains, or OUs to apply configurations such as security settings, software installation policies, and login scripts.

To create a new GPO using CLI commands, administrators can use the **New-GPO** cmdlet in PowerShell:

sqlCopy code

```
New-GPO -Name "Account Lockout Policy"
```

This command creates a new GPO named "Account Lockout Policy" that can be linked to an appropriate container in Active Directory.

Global Catalog:

The Global Catalog (GC) is a distributed data repository that contains a partial replica of all objects in the forest. It facilitates searches for objects across domains within a forest and is used by applications and services to locate directory information efficiently.

To enable the Global Catalog on a domain controller using CLI commands, administrators can use the **Set-ADForest** cmdlet in PowerShell:

sqlCopy code

Set-ADForest -GlobalCatalogEnabled $true

This command enables the Global Catalog on the specified domain controller, allowing it to serve GC queries.

In summary, the core components and concepts of Active Directory provide the foundation for effective directory service management in Windows environments. Understanding domains, forests, OUs, GPOs, and the Global Catalog is essential for administrators tasked with deploying, configuring, and maintaining Active Directory environments. By leveraging CLI commands and PowerShell cmdlets, administrators can streamline tasks such as domain controller deployment, OU creation, GPO management, and Global Catalog configuration, ensuring efficient and secure directory service operation.

Chapter 2: Understanding Windows Network Architecture

Transmission Control Protocol/Internet Protocol (TCP/IP) is the fundamental networking protocol suite used for communication and data transfer in modern computer networks. Understanding TCP/IP fundamentals is crucial for anyone working in the field of networking, whether as a network administrator, engineer, or technician. Next, we will delve into the core concepts and components of TCP/IP, along with practical examples and CLI commands for deploying and configuring TCP/IP networks.

Overview of TCP/IP: TCP/IP is a suite of protocols that provides the foundation for communication across interconnected networks. It comprises multiple protocols, each serving a specific function in the data transmission process. The two primary protocols in the TCP/IP suite are Transmission Control Protocol (TCP) and Internet Protocol (IP). TCP ensures reliable, connection-oriented data delivery, while IP handles the addressing and routing of packets across networks.

IP Addressing: IP addressing is central to TCP/IP networks, as it enables devices to identify and communicate with each other. IPv4 (Internet Protocol version 4) and IPv6 (Internet Protocol version 6) are the two main versions of the IP protocol. IPv4 addresses consist of 32 bits, typically expressed in dotted-decimal notation (e.g., 192.168.1.1), while IPv6 addresses use 128 bits and are represented in hexadecimal format (e.g., 2001:0db8:85a3:0000:0000:8a2e:0370:7334).

To configure an IPv4 address on a network interface using the command-line interface, administrators can use the netsh command in Windows or the ip command in Unix-based systems. For example:

vbnetCopy code

netsh interface ipv4 set address "Ethernet" static 192.168.1.10 255.255.255.0

This command sets the IPv4 address of the "Ethernet" interface to 192.168.1.10 with a subnet mask of 255.255.255.0.

Subnetting and CIDR: Subnetting is the process of dividing a large network into smaller subnetworks to improve efficiency and manageability. Classless Inter-Domain Routing (CIDR) notation is commonly used to specify subnet masks and address ranges. CIDR notation consists of an IP address followed by a forward slash and a subnet mask length (e.g., 192.168.1.0/24).

To define a subnet using CIDR notation, administrators can use the ip command in Unix-based systems or the netsh command in Windows. For example:

csharpCopy code

ip address add 192.168.1.1/24 dev eth0

This command adds the IP address 192.168.1.1 with a subnet mask of 255.255.255.0 to the "eth0" network interface.

Routing: Routing is the process of directing network traffic between different subnets or networks. Routers use routing tables to determine the best path for forwarding packets based on destination IP addresses. Static routing involves manually configuring routing entries, while dynamic routing protocols such as Routing Information Protocol (RIP) and Open Shortest Path First (OSPF) automate the exchange of routing information between routers.

To add a static route using the route command in Windows, administrators can use a command similar to the following:
csharpCopy code
route add 10.0.0.0 mask 255.0.0.0 192.168.1.1
This command adds a static route for the 10.0.0.0/8 network via the gateway 192.168.1.1.

Domain Name System (DNS): DNS is a distributed naming system that translates domain names into IP addresses, allowing users to access resources on the internet using human-readable names. DNS servers maintain databases called zone files, which contain mappings between domain names and IP addresses.

To configure DNS settings on a Windows machine using CLI commands, administrators can use the netsh command. For example:
vbnetCopy code
netsh interface ipv4 set dns "Ethernet" static 8.8.8.8
This command sets the DNS server address for the "Ethernet" interface to 8.8.8.8.

Dynamic Host Configuration Protocol (DHCP): DHCP is a network protocol used to automatically assign IP addresses and other network configuration parameters to devices on a network. DHCP servers lease IP addresses to clients for a specified period, simplifying network administration and management.

To configure a DHCP server on a Windows Server using PowerShell commands, administrators can use the Install-WindowsFeature cmdlet to install the DHCP Server role, followed by the Add-DhcpServerv4Scope cmdlet to create a new DHCP scope. For example:
mathematicaCopy code

Install-WindowsFeature -Name DHCP -IncludeManagementTools Add-DhcpServerv4Scope -Name "LAN" -StartRange 192.168.1.100 -EndRange 192.168.1.200 -SubnetMask 255.255.255.0 -State Active This sequence of commands installs the DHCP Server role and creates a new DHCP scope named "LAN" with an address range from 192.168.1.100 to 192.168.1.200.

In summary, TCP/IP fundamentals form the cornerstone of modern networking, enabling communication and data transfer across diverse networks. Understanding IP addressing, subnetting, routing, DNS, and DHCP is essential for designing, deploying, and troubleshooting TCP/IP-based networks. By leveraging CLI commands and practical examples, network administrators can effectively configure and manage TCP/IP networks to meet the demands of today's interconnected world.

In the realm of network administration, understanding the concepts of domains, workgroups, and forests is essential. These concepts form the foundation of organizational structure and resource management in Windows-based environments. Next, we will explore the definitions, roles, and deployment strategies associated with domains, workgroups, and forests, along with practical examples and CLI commands for implementing these concepts effectively.

Workgroup: A workgroup is a basic peer-to-peer network configuration where computers are connected without centralized control. In a workgroup environment, each computer manages its own resources and security settings independently, without relying on a central server. Workgroups are typically used in small-scale environments where simplicity and flexibility are prioritized over centralized management. To configure a workgroup on a Windows computer using CLI commands, administrators can use the net command to set the workgroup name. For example:

arduinoCopy code

```
net                    config                    workstation
/WORKGROUP:WORKGROUP_NAME
```

This command sets the workgroup name to "WORKGROUP_NAME" on the local workstation.

Domain: A domain is a centralized network configuration where computers, users, and resources are managed and authenticated by a domain controller. Domains provide centralized user authentication, access control, and resource management, allowing administrators to enforce security policies and streamline network administration tasks. Domains are commonly used in medium to large-scale environments where security, scalability, and centralized management are essential.

To join a Windows computer to a domain using CLI commands, administrators can use the netdom command. For example:

bashCopy code

```
netdom              join              COMPUTER_NAME
/Domain:DOMAIN_NAME              /UserD:USERNAME
/PasswordD:PASSWORD
```

This command joins the computer named "COMPUTER_NAME" to the domain specified by "DOMAIN_NAME" using the credentials provided. **Forest:** A forest is a collection of one or more domains that share a common schema, configuration, and global catalog. Forests enable organizations to establish trust relationships between domains and consolidate resources across multiple domains. Each domain within a forest maintains its own security policies and administrative boundaries while benefiting from the shared resources and trust relationships established at the forest level.

To create a new forest using CLI commands, administrators can use the dcpromo command on a Windows Server. For example:

rubyCopy code

```
dcpromo                                    /unattend
/ForestLevel:DOMAIN_FUNCTIONAL_LEVEL
/DomainLevel:DOMAIN_FUNCTIONAL_LEVEL
/DatabasePath:"C:\Windows\NTDS"
/LogPath:"C:\Windows\NTDS"
/SysVolPath:"C:\Windows\SYSVOL"
```

This command initiates an unattended installation of a domain controller and prompts the administrator to specify the forest and domain functional levels, along with the paths for the database, log files, and SysVol folder.

Trust Relationships: Trust relationships establish secure communication and resource sharing between domains within a forest or across different forests. Trust relationships can be one-way or two-way, depending on the direction of trust and the level of authentication required. By establishing trust relationships, administrators can grant users in one domain access to resources in another domain without the need for separate authentication. To create a trust relationship between two domains using CLI commands, administrators can use the Netdom command in Windows. For example:

```ruby
rubyCopy code
netdom              trust              DOMAIN_NAME1
/Domain:DOMAIN_NAME2 /Add
```
This command establishes a one-way trust relationship where DOMAIN_NAME1 trusts DOMAIN_NAME2.

In summary, understanding the concepts of domains, workgroups, and forests is crucial for effective network administration in Windows environments. Whether deploying a small-scale peer-to-peer network or managing a large-scale domain infrastructure, administrators must consider the implications of these concepts on security, scalability, and centralized management. By leveraging CLI commands and practical examples, administrators can deploy and manage domains, workgroups, and forests with confidence, ensuring the stability and security of their network environments.

Chapter 3: Installing and Configuring Active Directory

Before embarking on the installation of Active Directory (AD), it's crucial to ensure that thorough preparation is undertaken. Active Directory serves as the foundation for centralized network management, authentication, and access control in Windows environments. Proper preparation ensures a smooth deployment process and lays the groundwork for a stable and secure AD infrastructure. Next, we will explore the key steps and considerations involved in preparing for Active Directory installation, accompanied by practical examples and CLI commands where applicable.

Assessing Infrastructure Requirements: The first step in preparing for Active Directory installation is to assess the infrastructure requirements. This involves evaluating factors such as network topology, hardware specifications, and software compatibility. Ensure that the hardware meets the minimum requirements for running Active Directory Domain Services (AD DS) and that all necessary software dependencies are installed and up to date.

Planning Active Directory Domain Structure: A critical aspect of Active Directory preparation is planning the domain structure. Define the desired domain hierarchy, including the number of domains and their relationships (e.g., parent-child domains, trust relationships). Consider factors such as organizational structure, administrative boundaries, and scalability requirements. Document the domain structure plan to serve as a reference during the installation process.

Network Configuration and DNS Setup: Active Directory heavily relies on DNS for name resolution and service location. Ensure that the network is properly configured with DNS servers that support dynamic updates and are capable of resolving AD-specific DNS queries. Configure the network adapters of domain controllers with static IP addresses and appropriate DNS settings to prevent issues during AD installation.

To configure a static IP address on a Windows Server using CLI commands, administrators can use the netsh command. For example:

vbnetCopy code

```
netsh interface ipv4 set address "Local Area Connection" static 192.168.1.10 255.255.255.0
```

This command sets the IPv4 address of the "Local Area Connection" interface to 192.168.1.10 with a subnet mask of 255.255.255.0.

Domain Controller Hardware and Software Preparation: Ensure that the hardware designated for domain controllers meets the recommended specifications for running Active Directory. Verify that the server operating system is compatible with the desired version of Active Directory and that all prerequisite software components are installed. Prepare the server by installing the necessary roles and features, such as Active Directory Domain Services (AD DS).

To install the AD DS role on a Windows Server using PowerShell commands, administrators can use the Install-WindowsFeature cmdlet. For example:

mathematicaCopy code

```
Install-WindowsFeature -Name AD-Domain-Services -IncludeManagementTools
```

This command installs the AD DS role and includes the management tools necessary for configuring and managing Active Directory.

Active Directory Site Design: Active Directory sites represent physical or logical network segments connected by high-speed links. Plan the site topology based on factors such as geographic location, network bandwidth, and replication requirements. Define sites, site links, and site link bridges to optimize replication traffic and ensure efficient communication between domain controllers.

Security Considerations: Security should be a primary consideration when preparing for Active Directory installation. Review security best practices and guidelines provided by Microsoft, and implement appropriate measures to safeguard the AD environment. This may include configuring firewalls, enabling auditing and logging, and implementing strong password policies.

Backup and Recovery Planning: Develop a comprehensive backup and recovery plan to protect against data loss and ensure business continuity. Establish regular backup schedules for critical AD components, including domain controllers, DNS zones, and Group Policy objects. Test the backup and recovery procedures to verify their effectiveness in restoring AD services in the event of a disaster.

In summary, preparing for Active Directory installation requires careful planning and consideration of various factors, including infrastructure requirements, domain structure, network configuration, hardware and software preparation, site design, security, and backup and recovery planning. By following best practices and leveraging CLI commands and practical examples, administrators can streamline the preparation process and lay the groundwork for a successful Active Directory deployment.

Installing Active Directory (AD) is a critical task for network administrators tasked with deploying and managing Windows-based environments. Active Directory serves as the cornerstone of centralized network management, providing authentication, authorization, and directory services. A step-by-step installation guide ensures a smooth and successful deployment of Active Directory, laying the foundation for a secure and efficient network infrastructure. Next, we will provide a comprehensive walkthrough of the Active Directory installation process, accompanied by practical examples and CLI commands where applicable.

Pre-installation Tasks: Before initiating the Active Directory installation process, ensure that all prerequisite tasks have been completed. This includes assessing infrastructure requirements, planning the domain structure, configuring network settings, preparing domain controller hardware and software, designing Active Directory sites, and addressing security considerations. Take the time to review documentation and best practices provided by Microsoft to ensure a successful deployment.

Launching Server Manager: Begin the Active Directory installation process by launching Server Manager, the management console used for configuring and managing server roles and features in Windows Server operating systems. Server Manager provides a centralized interface for installing and configuring Active Directory Domain Services (AD DS) and other server roles.

To launch Server Manager from the command line interface (CLI) on a Windows Server, administrators can use the servermanagercmd command. For example:

Copy code

```
servermanagercmd -install AD-Domain-Services
```

This command installs the AD DS role on the local server using the Server Manager command-line interface.

Adding Roles and Features: In Server Manager, navigate to the "Manage" menu and select "Add Roles and Features" to initiate the role installation wizard. Follow the prompts to select the server on which to install Active Directory Domain Services and proceed to the "Features" section. Ensure that the necessary features, such as Group Policy Management and DNS Server, are selected for installation to support Active Directory functionality.

Installing Active Directory Domain Services: In the "Select Server Roles" section of the role installation wizard, select "Active Directory Domain Services" as the role to install. Review the role description and click "Next" to proceed. Confirm any additional role services or features required for AD DS, such as DNS Server, and click "Next" to begin the installation process.

To install the AD DS role using PowerShell commands, administrators can use the Install-WindowsFeature cmdlet. For example:

mathematicaCopy code

```
Install-WindowsFeature -Name AD-Domain-Services -IncludeManagementTools
```

This command installs the AD DS role and includes the management tools necessary for configuring and managing Active Directory.

Configuring Active Directory Domain Services: Once the AD DS role installation is complete, proceed to configure Active Directory Domain Services using the "Active Directory Domain Services Configuration Wizard." Follow the prompts to specify whether to add a new forest, add a domain to an existing forest, or create a new domain in an existing forest.

To launch the Active Directory Domain Services Configuration Wizard from the command line interface, administrators can use the dcpromo command. For example:

```ruby
rubyCopy code
dcpromo /unattend /ForestLevel:Windows2016Forest
/DomainLevel:Windows2016Domain
/DatabasePath:"C:\Windows\NTDS"
/LogPath:"C:\Windows\NTDS"
/SysVolPath:"C:\Windows\SYSVOL"
```

This command initiates an unattended installation of a domain controller and prompts the administrator to specify the forest and domain functional levels, along with the paths for the database, log files, and SysVol folder.

Completing the Installation: Follow the prompts in the Active Directory Domain Services Configuration Wizard to specify the domain and forest names, as well as the Directory Services Restore Mode (DSRM) password. Review the configuration settings and click "Next" to begin the installation process. Once the installation is complete, restart the server to finalize the Active Directory deployment.

To restart the server from the command line interface, administrators can use the shutdown command with the -r option. For example:

bashCopy code

shutdown /r /t 0

This command restarts the server immediately (/t 0) after displaying a message indicating the restart.

Post-installation Tasks: After completing the Active Directory installation, perform post-installation tasks to verify the successful deployment and configure additional settings as needed. This may include configuring DNS settings, verifying replication status, creating organizational units (OUs) and group policies, and configuring security settings.

In summary, a step-by-step installation guide for Active Directory ensures a smooth and successful deployment of this critical network infrastructure component. By following the outlined process and leveraging CLI commands and practical examples, administrators can deploy Active Directory with confidence, laying the foundation for a secure and efficient network environment.

Chapter 4: Managing Users and Groups

User Account Management is a crucial aspect of maintaining a secure and efficient network environment. In any organization, user accounts are the primary means by which individuals access network resources and perform their roles and responsibilities. Effective user account management involves creating, modifying, and deleting user accounts, as well as assigning appropriate permissions and security settings. Next, we will explore the key principles and techniques of user account management, accompanied by practical examples and CLI commands where applicable.

Creating User Accounts: The first step in user account management is creating user accounts for individuals who require access to the network. User accounts typically include a username, password, and other attributes such as email address, department, and job title. In Windows environments, user accounts can be created using the Active Directory Users and Computers (ADUC) console or PowerShell commands.

To create a user account using PowerShell commands, administrators can use the New-ADUser cmdlet. For example:

```perl
perlCopy code
New-ADUser -Name "John Smith" -SamAccountName "jsmith" -UserPrincipalName "jsmith@contoso.com" -AccountPassword (ConvertTo-SecureString "Password123" -AsPlainText -Force) -Enabled $true
```

This command creates a new user account named "John Smith" with the username "jsmith" and email address "jsmith@contoso.com", and sets the password to "Password123".

Modifying User Accounts: User accounts may need to be modified over time due to changes in roles, responsibilities, or personal information. Common modifications include updating contact information, changing passwords, and adjusting group memberships. Administrators can modify user accounts using the ADUC console or PowerShell commands.

To modify a user account using PowerShell commands, administrators can use the Set-ADUser cmdlet. For example:

mathematicaCopy code

```
Set-ADUser -Identity "jsmith" -Department "Finance" -Office "Office123" -Description "Senior Financial Analyst"
```

This command updates the department, office, and description attributes of the user account with the username "jsmith".

Resetting Passwords: Password resets are a common task in user account management, especially in cases where users forget their passwords or security concerns arise. Administrators can reset user passwords using the ADUC console, PowerShell commands, or the net user command in Windows.

To reset a user password using PowerShell commands, administrators can use the Set-ADAccountPassword cmdlet. For example:

mathematicaCopy code

```
Set-ADAccountPassword -Identity "jsmith" -Reset -NewPassword (ConvertTo-SecureString "NewPassword123" -AsPlainText -Force)
```

This command resets the password for the user account with the username "jsmith" to "NewPassword123".

Disabling and Enabling User Accounts: User accounts may need to be disabled temporarily (e.g., during employee leave) or permanently (e.g., upon termination). Disabling a user account prevents the user from accessing network resources while retaining their account information. Administrators can disable and enable user accounts using the ADUC console or PowerShell commands.

To disable a user account using PowerShell commands, administrators can use the Disable-ADAccount cmdlet. For example:

mathematicaCopy code

```
Disable-ADAccount -Identity "jsmith"
```

This command disables the user account with the username "jsmith".

Deleting User Accounts: When users leave the organization or are no longer required to access network resources, their user accounts should be deleted to maintain security and compliance. Administrators can delete user accounts using the ADUC console or PowerShell commands.

To delete a user account using PowerShell commands, administrators can use the Remove-ADUser cmdlet. For example:

mathematicaCopy code

```
Remove-ADUser -Identity "jsmith" -Confirm:$false
```

This command deletes the user account with the username "jsmith" without prompting for confirmation.

Group Memberships: Group memberships play a vital role in user account management, as they determine the resources and permissions users have access to. Administrators can add or remove users from groups using the ADUC console or PowerShell commands.

To add a user to a group using PowerShell commands, administrators can use the Add-ADGroupMember cmdlet. For example:

sqlCopy code

Add-ADGroupMember -Identity "FinanceGroup" -Members "jsmith"

This command adds the user with the username "jsmith" to the group named "FinanceGroup".

In summary, effective user account management is essential for maintaining a secure and efficient network environment. By following best practices and leveraging CLI commands and practical examples, administrators can create, modify, and manage user accounts with confidence, ensuring that users have the appropriate access to network resources while maintaining security and compliance.

Group management plays a crucial role in organizing users, simplifying access control, and enhancing security within an organization's network environment. By effectively managing groups, administrators can streamline user permissions, enforce consistent security policies, and facilitate collaboration among users with similar roles or responsibilities. Next, we will delve into the fundamentals of group management, explore best practices for group administration, and provide practical examples along with CLI commands where applicable.

Understanding Groups: Groups are collections of user accounts, computer accounts, or other groups that share common permissions and access rights to resources within the network. There are two main types of groups in Active Directory: security groups and distribution groups. Security groups are used to control access to resources, while distribution groups are used for email distribution purposes.

Creating Groups: Group creation is typically performed using administrative tools such as Active Directory Users and Computers (ADUC) or PowerShell commands. When creating groups, it's essential to follow naming conventions and establish clear group membership criteria to ensure consistency and manageability.

To create a new security group using PowerShell commands, administrators can use the **New-ADGroup** cmdlet. For example:

sqlCopy code

```
New-ADGroup -Name "FinanceGroup" -GroupScope Global -GroupCategory Security -Path "OU=Groups,DC=example,DC=com"
```

This command creates a new security group named "FinanceGroup" in the specified organizational unit (OU) within the Active Directory domain.

Managing Group Membership: Group membership should be regularly reviewed and updated to reflect changes in user roles, responsibilities, and organizational structure. Administrators can add or remove users from groups using administrative tools or PowerShell commands.

To add a user to a group using PowerShell commands, administrators can use the **Add-ADGroupMember** cmdlet. For example:

sqlCopy code

```
Add-ADGroupMember -Identity "FinanceGroup" -Members "jsmith"
```

This command adds the user with the username "jsmith" to the "FinanceGroup" security group.

Implementing Group Nesting: Group nesting involves nesting one group within another to simplify access control and permission assignment. By nesting groups, administrators can apply permissions to parent groups, which are inherited by nested groups and their members.

To nest a group within another group using PowerShell commands, administrators can use the **Add-ADGroupMember** cmdlet. For example:

```sql
sqlCopy code
Add-ADGroupMember -Identity "ParentGroup" -Members
"ChildGroup"
```

This command nests the group named "ChildGroup" within the group named "ParentGroup".

Best Practices for Group Management: When managing groups, it's essential to adhere to best practices to ensure efficient administration and maintain security. Some best practices for group management include:

Establishing a clear naming convention for groups to reflect their purpose and membership criteria.

Regularly reviewing and auditing group memberships to ensure accuracy and compliance with organizational policies.

Limiting the number of group memberships per user to prevent excessive access privileges and simplify permissions management.

Documenting group membership and access control policies to facilitate troubleshooting and compliance audits.

Implementing role-based access control (RBAC) by assigning permissions to groups based on users' roles and responsibilities.

Delegating group management tasks to designated administrators or group owners to distribute administrative responsibilities and enhance accountability.

Group Policy Management: Group Policy Objects (GPOs) are used to enforce security settings, configurations, and restrictions across Active Directory domains. Group Policy management is essential for maintaining consistent security posture and enforcing organizational policies.

To manage group policies, administrators can use the Group Policy Management Console (GPMC) or PowerShell commands. For example, to create a new GPO using PowerShell:

sqlCopy code

```
New-GPO -Name "Account Lockout Policy"
```

This command creates a new GPO named "Account Lockout Policy" that can be linked to an appropriate organizational unit (OU) in Active Directory.

Monitoring and Auditing: Regular monitoring and auditing of group memberships, permissions, and access events are essential for detecting unauthorized access attempts and ensuring compliance with security policies. Administrators can use tools such as Windows Event Viewer and audit policies to monitor group-related activities and security events.

To enable auditing of group membership changes in Active Directory, administrators can configure audit policies using Group Policy. For example, to audit changes to group membership:

mathematicaCopy code

```
Set-ItemProperty                     -Path
"HKLM:\System\CurrentControlSet\Services\NTDS\Paramet
ers" -Name "Audit\Directory Service Access" -Value 3
```

This command configures the Directory Service Access audit policy to log changes to group memberships.

In summary, effective group management is essential for maintaining a secure, efficient, and well-organized network environment. By following best practices and leveraging administrative tools and PowerShell commands, administrators can streamline group administration, enforce security policies, and facilitate collaboration among users and resources within the organization.

Chapter 5: Group Policy Fundamentals

Group Policy Objects (GPOs) are a fundamental component of the Microsoft Windows operating system's Active Directory infrastructure. They enable administrators to manage and enforce various settings, configurations, and policies across a network of computers and users. GPOs provide a centralized and efficient method for controlling security settings, desktop configurations, application settings, and more. Next, we will delve into the fundamentals of Group Policy Objects, explore their capabilities, and discuss practical examples along with CLI commands where applicable.

Understanding Group Policy Objects: A Group Policy Object (GPO) is a container for Group Policy settings that are applied to user objects and computer objects within Active Directory domains. GPOs allow administrators to define and enforce configurations and policies at the domain, site, or organizational unit (OU) level. These policies are then applied to users and computers based on their location within the Active Directory hierarchy.

Creating and Managing GPOs: GPOs can be created and managed using the Group Policy Management Console (GPMC) or PowerShell commands. Administrators can create new GPOs, link them to specific OUs, configure policy settings, and delegate management tasks as needed.

To create a new GPO using PowerShell commands, administrators can use the New-GPO cmdlet. For example: sqlCopy code

New-GPO -Name "Account Lockout Policy"

This command creates a new GPO named "Account Lockout Policy" that can be configured to enforce account lockout settings across the domain.

Linking GPOs to Active Directory Objects: After creating a GPO, administrators must link it to the appropriate Active Directory objects (e.g., domain, site, OU) to apply the configured policy settings. GPOs can be linked to multiple containers within the Active Directory hierarchy to target specific sets of users and computers.

To link a GPO to an organizational unit (OU) using PowerShell commands, administrators can use the New-GPLink cmdlet. For example:

sqlCopy code

```
New-GPLink -Name "Account Lockout Policy" -Target "OU=Finance,DC=contoso,DC=com"
```

This command links the "Account Lockout Policy" GPO to the "Finance" organizational unit within the contoso.com domain.

Configuring GPO Settings: GPO settings are organized into two categories: Computer Configuration and User Configuration. Computer Configuration settings apply to computer objects, while User Configuration settings apply to user objects. Administrators can configure a wide range of settings within each category, including security settings, registry settings, software installation policies, and more.

To configure GPO settings using the Group Policy Management Console (GPMC), administrators can navigate to the desired GPO, right-click, and select "Edit" to open the Group Policy Object Editor. From there, they can navigate through the available policy settings and configure them according to their requirements.

Enforcing and Blocking GPO Inheritance: GPOs are processed in a hierarchical manner, with settings from higher-level GPOs being inherited by lower-level objects unless explicitly blocked or overwritten. Administrators can enforce or block GPO inheritance to control which GPO settings are applied to specific containers within the Active Directory hierarchy.

To enforce a GPO at a specific level using PowerShell commands, administrators can use the Set-GPInheritance cmdlet. For example:

sqlCopy code

Set-GPInheritance -Name "Account Lockout Policy" -Target "OU=Finance,DC=contoso,DC=com" -IsEnforced:$true

This command enforces the "Account Lockout Policy" GPO at the "Finance" organizational unit level, ensuring that its settings are applied even if blocked by higher-level GPOs.

Filtering GPO Application: Administrators can use security filtering and WMI filtering to further refine the scope of GPO application based on security group membership or system attributes. This allows for more granular control over which users and computers receive specific GPO settings.

To apply a GPO only to members of a specific security group using PowerShell commands, administrators can use the Set-GPPermission cmdlet. For example:

sqlCopy code

Set-GPPermission -Name "Account Lockout Policy" -PermissionLevel GpoApply -TargetName "Finance Group" -TargetType Group -AuthType All

This command grants the "Finance Group" security group permission to apply the "Account Lockout Policy" GPO.

Troubleshooting GPO Application: If GPO settings are not being applied as expected, administrators can use tools such as Group Policy Results (GPResult) and Group Policy Modeling to diagnose and troubleshoot GPO processing issues. These tools provide detailed reports on which GPOs are being applied and why.

To generate a Group Policy Results report for a specific user and computer combination using CLI commands, administrators can use the gpresult command. For example: bashCopy code

gpresult /user jsmith /scope computer /v

This command generates a verbose Group Policy Results report for the user "jsmith" on the local computer, displaying all applied and denied GPOs.

In summary, Group Policy Objects (GPOs) are powerful tools for managing and enforcing configurations and policies within Active Directory environments. By understanding the fundamentals of GPOs and leveraging administrative tools and PowerShell commands, administrators can efficiently configure and manage GPOs to maintain a secure, consistent, and well-managed network infrastructure.

Group Policy is a powerful tool in Windows environments that allows administrators to centrally manage and enforce settings, configurations, and security policies across a network of computers and users. Understanding how Group Policy processing and application work is essential for administrators to effectively manage and maintain a secure and consistent network environment. Next, we will explore the intricacies of Group Policy processing and application, including the various stages involved, troubleshooting techniques, and practical examples with CLI commands where applicable.

Introduction to Group Policy Processing: Group Policy processing refers to the series of steps that occur when a computer or user logs on to the network and receives Group Policy settings. The process involves multiple stages, including discovery, retrieval, and application of Group Policy objects (GPOs). Understanding these stages is crucial for administrators to ensure that desired policies are applied correctly.

Group Policy Processing Phases: Group Policy processing occurs in two main phases: computer startup and user logon. During computer startup, Group Policy settings that apply to computer objects are processed, while during user logon, Group Policy settings that apply to user objects are processed. Each phase consists of several sub-phases, including discovery, processing, and application of GPOs.

Discovery and Retrieval of GPOs: The first stage of Group Policy processing involves the discovery and retrieval of GPOs that are linked to the computer or user object. This process involves querying Active Directory to identify the GPOs that apply to the object based on its location in the Active Directory hierarchy.

To manually retrieve the list of GPOs that apply to a computer using CLI commands, administrators can use the gpresult command. For example:

bashCopy code

```
gpresult /r /scope computer
```

This command displays the list of GPOs that apply to the current computer.

Processing and Application of GPOs: Once the list of applicable GPOs has been retrieved, Group Policy processing proceeds to the next stage, where the settings within each GPO are processed and applied to the computer or user. This process involves evaluating each setting within the GPO and applying it to the appropriate registry keys or policy areas.

To view the settings within a specific GPO using the Group Policy Management Console (GPMC), administrators can navigate to the GPO, right-click, and select "Edit" to open the Group Policy Object Editor. From there, they can navigate through the available policy settings and review their configurations.

GPO Inheritance and Precedence: Group Policy processing takes into account the inheritance and precedence of GPOs within the Active Directory hierarchy. GPOs linked to higher-level containers (e.g., domain or site) are processed before GPOs linked to lower-level containers (e.g., OU). In addition, GPOs with higher precedence (e.g., enforced GPOs) take precedence over GPOs with lower precedence.

To enforce a GPO at a specific level using CLI commands, administrators can use the Set-GPInheritance cmdlet. For example:

sqlCopy code

Set-GPInheritance -Name "Account Lockout Policy" -Target "OU=Finance,DC=contoso,DC=com" -IsEnforced:$true

This command enforces the "Account Lockout Policy" GPO at the "Finance" organizational unit level.

Filtering GPO Application: Administrators can use security filtering and WMI filtering to further refine the scope of GPO application based on security group membership or system attributes. This allows for more granular control over which users and computers receive specific GPO settings.

To apply a GPO only to members of a specific security group using CLI commands, administrators can use the Set-GPPermission cmdlet. For example:

sqlCopy code

Set-GPPermission -Name "Account Lockout Policy" -PermissionLevel GpoApply -TargetName "Finance Group" -TargetType Group -AuthType All

This command grants the "Finance Group" security group permission to apply the "Account Lockout Policy" GPO.

Troubleshooting Group Policy Processing: If Group Policy settings are not being applied as expected, administrators can use tools such as Group Policy Results (GPResult) and Group Policy Modeling to diagnose and troubleshoot processing issues. These tools provide detailed reports on which GPOs are being applied and why.

To generate a Group Policy Results report for a specific user and computer combination using CLI commands, administrators can use the gpresult command. For example:

bashCopy code

gpresult /user jsmith /scope computer /v

This command generates a verbose Group Policy Results report for the user "jsmith" on the local computer, displaying all applied and denied GPOs.

In summary, understanding Group Policy processing and application is essential for administrators to effectively manage and maintain a secure and consistent network environment. By understanding the stages of Group Policy processing, GPO inheritance and precedence, and troubleshooting techniques, administrators can ensure that desired policies are applied correctly and consistently across their network.

Chapter 6: File and Print Services Integration

File services are a critical component of network infrastructure, facilitating the storage, organization, and access of files and folders within an organization. In Windows environments, Active Directory (AD) plays a central role in managing file services, providing capabilities for centralized authentication, access control, and resource management. Configuring file services in Active Directory involves various tasks, including setting up file shares, configuring permissions, implementing quotas, and enabling access auditing. Next, we will explore the process of configuring file services in Active Directory, discussing best practices, practical examples, and CLI commands where applicable.

Introduction to File Services: File services encompass a range of functionalities aimed at managing and sharing files and folders within a network. These services include file sharing, access control, storage management, and data protection. In Active Directory environments, file services are often integrated with AD to leverage centralized user authentication and authorization.

Setting Up File Shares: File shares are directories or folders on a file server that are made available to network users for accessing and storing files. To create a file share in Windows Server, administrators can use the File and Storage Services role and the Server Manager console. Alternatively, they can use PowerShell commands for automated deployment.

To create a new file share using PowerShell commands, administrators can use the New-SmbShare cmdlet. For example:

mathematicaCopy code

```
New-SmbShare -Name "DataShare" -Path "C:\Data" -
FullAccess "Domain Users"
```
This command creates a new file share named "DataShare" on the "C:\Data" directory with full access granted to all domain users.

Configuring Share Permissions: Share permissions control access to file shares at the network level, specifying which users and groups have permission to access the share. Share permissions are typically configured in conjunction with NTFS permissions to provide comprehensive access control.

To configure share permissions using the Server Manager console, administrators can navigate to the properties of the file share and adjust the permissions under the "Share" tab. Alternatively, they can use PowerShell commands with the Set-SmbShare cmdlet to modify share permissions.

javascriptCopy code

```
Set-SmbShare        -Name       "DataShare"       -
FolderEnumerationMode AccessBased
```
This command configures the "DataShare" file share to use Access-Based Enumeration, which hides files and folders from users who do not have permission to access them.

Configuring NTFS Permissions: NTFS permissions govern access to files and folders at the file system level, determining which users and groups can read, write, modify, or delete files and folders. NTFS permissions are applied directly to files and folders and are independent of share permissions.

To configure NTFS permissions using the File Explorer interface, administrators can navigate to the properties of a file or folder, select the "Security" tab, and adjust the permissions accordingly. Alternatively, they can use PowerShell commands with the Get-Acl and Set-Acl cmdlets to manage NTFS permissions programmatically.

mathematicaCopy code

```
Get-Acl -Path "C:\Data" | Set-Acl -Path "C:\Data" -AccessControl
```

This command retrieves the current ACL (Access Control List) for the "C:\Data" directory and applies it back to the same directory, effectively resetting the permissions to their default state.

Implementing Quotas: Quotas allow administrators to limit the amount of disk space that users or groups can consume on a file server. Quotas help prevent users from monopolizing storage resources and ensure equitable distribution of disk space.

To configure disk quotas using the File Server Resource Manager (FSRM) in Windows Server, administrators can open the FSRM console, navigate to the Quota Management section, and create new quotas for specific volumes or folders. Alternatively, they can use PowerShell commands with the New-FsrmQuota cmdlet to automate quota configuration.

mathematicaCopy code

```
New-FsrmQuota -Path "C:\Data" -Description "User Quota" -Size 1GB -Template "UserQuota"
```

This command creates a new quota on the "C:\Data" directory with a limit of 1GB, applying the "UserQuota" template to enforce quota settings.

Enabling Access Auditing: Access auditing allows administrators to track and monitor access to files and folders, helping to detect unauthorized access attempts and ensure compliance with security policies. Auditing can capture events such as file access, permission changes, and file deletions.

To enable access auditing using Group Policy in Active Directory, administrators can configure audit policies at the domain or organizational unit level using the Group Policy

Management Console. They can specify which types of access events to audit and which users or groups to audit.

bashCopy code

```
Auditpol /set /subcategory: "File System" /success: enable /failure: enable
```

This command enables auditing for file system access events, allowing the system to log successful and failed access attempts.

Monitoring and Reporting: After configuring file services, it's important to monitor and analyze file server activity to identify potential security risks, performance issues, and compliance violations. Administrators can use tools such as Windows Event Viewer, PowerShell scripts, and third-party monitoring solutions to monitor file server activity and generate reports.

mathematicaCopy code

```
Get-WinEvent -LogName Security -FilterXPath "*[System[(EventID=4663)]]" | Format-List
```

This PowerShell command retrieves security events related to file access (Event ID 4663) from the Security event log and formats the output as a list for easy analysis.

In summary, configuring file services in Active Directory involves a series of tasks aimed at providing secure, efficient, and manageable file sharing capabilities within an organization. By following best practices and leveraging administrative tools and PowerShell commands, administrators can configure file shares, manage permissions, implement quotas, enable access auditing, and monitor file server activity effectively. This ensures that users have access to the resources they need while maintaining the security and integrity of the organization's data.

Print services and printer management are essential components of network infrastructure, enabling users to print documents from their computers to shared printers across the network. In Windows environments, Active Directory (AD) plays a crucial role in managing print services, providing centralized printer deployment, configuration, and access control. This chapter explores the configuration and management of print services and printers in Active Directory, covering best practices, practical examples, and CLI commands where applicable.

Introduction to Print Services: Print services facilitate the printing of documents from computers to printers connected to the network. In Windows environments, print services are typically provided by a print server, which hosts shared printers and manages print jobs. Active Directory integration allows for centralized management of printers, simplifying deployment and access control.

Setting Up a Print Server: To set up a print server in Windows Server, administrators can install the Print and Document Services role using the Server Manager console. Once installed, they can configure printers, printer drivers, and print queues on the print server.

mathematicaCopy code

```
Add-WindowsFeature  Print-Services
```

This PowerShell command installs the Print and Document Services role on the current server.

Adding Printers to Active Directory: Active Directory integration allows administrators to publish printers in AD, making them easily discoverable by users and simplifying printer deployment. Printers can be added to AD manually or using PowerShell commands.

sqlCopy code

`Add-Printer -Name "Printer1" -DriverName "HP Universal Printing PCL 6" -PortName "IP_192.168.1.100"`

This command adds a printer named "Printer1" with the specified printer driver and port.

Deploying Printers via Group Policy: Group Policy can be used to deploy printers to users or computers within an Active Directory domain automatically. This method ensures that users have access to the necessary printers based on their location, department, or role.

To deploy printers via Group Policy, administrators can create a new Group Policy Object (GPO), navigate to the "User Configuration" or "Computer Configuration" section, and configure printer deployment settings under "Preferences" or "Policies".

Managing Printer Permissions: Printer permissions control who can access and use a printer. By default, only administrators and print operators have permissions to manage printers. Administrators can grant additional permissions to specific users or groups as needed.

To manage printer permissions using PowerShell, administrators can use the Set-Printer cmdlet. For example:

cssCopy code

`Set-Printer -Name "Printer1" -PermissionSDDL "D:PAI(A;;FA;;;BA)(A;;FR;;;BU)"`

This command grants full access to the printer named "Printer1" for the built-in administrators group and read access for all authenticated users.

Monitoring and Managing Print Queues: Print queues represent the list of print jobs waiting to be processed by a printer. Administrators can monitor and manage print queues to ensure efficient printing and troubleshoot printing issues.

To view print queues on a print server using PowerShell, administrators can use the Get-Printer cmdlet. For example:

vbnetCopy code

```
Get-Printer | Where-Object {$_.PrinterStatus -eq "Printing"}
```

This command retrieves a list of printers with print jobs currently in progress.

Implementing Printer Security: Printer security involves securing printers and print services to prevent unauthorized access and ensure the confidentiality and integrity of printed documents. This includes securing print queues, configuring printer encryption, and implementing secure printing solutions.

Administrators can configure printer security settings using the Print Management console or PowerShell commands. For example, to enable printer encryption:

sqlCopy code

```
Set-PrinterProperty -Name "Printer1" -EncryptionEnabled $true
```

This command enables encryption for the printer named "Printer1".

Printer Driver Management: Printer drivers are software components that allow computers to communicate with printers and generate print jobs. Administrators must ensure that the correct printer drivers are installed on print servers and client computers to ensure compatibility and reliable printing.

To manage printer drivers on a print server using PowerShell, administrators can use the Get-PrinterDriver and Add-PrinterDriver cmdlets. For example:

sqlCopy code

Get-PrinterDriver -Name "HP Universal Printing PCL 6" Add-PrinterDriver -Name "HP Universal Printing PCL 6" -InfPath "C:\Drivers\HPUPD.inf"

These commands retrieve information about the HP Universal Printing PCL 6 driver and install it on the print server.

In summary, print services and printer management are critical components of network infrastructure in Windows environments. By leveraging Active Directory integration, Group Policy deployment, PowerShell automation, and best practices in printer security and driver management, administrators can ensure efficient printing, streamline printer deployment, and maintain the integrity and security of printed documents across the organization.

Chapter 7: DNS and DHCP Configuration

Domain Name System (DNS) is a critical component of network infrastructure that translates human-readable domain names into IP addresses, allowing computers to communicate with each other over the internet or within a local network. In the context of Active Directory (AD), DNS plays a crucial role in providing name resolution services for AD domain controllers, clients, and resources. This chapter explores the fundamentals of DNS, its integration with Active Directory, best practices, and practical examples with CLI commands where applicable.

Understanding DNS Fundamentals: DNS is a hierarchical distributed database system that maps domain names to IP addresses. It comprises multiple DNS servers arranged in a hierarchical structure, with each server responsible for resolving domain names within its zone. DNS queries follow a recursive process, starting from the root DNS servers and traversing down to authoritative servers for the requested domain.

Installing and Configuring DNS Server: In Windows Server environments, DNS server functionality can be installed as a role using the Server Manager console or PowerShell commands.

mathematicaCopy code

```
Install-WindowsFeature -Name DNS -IncludeManagementTools
```

This PowerShell command installs the DNS Server role along with management tools on the current server.

After installation, administrators must configure DNS settings such as forwarders, zones, and recursion settings to ensure proper DNS resolution.

DNS Zones and Records: DNS zones are administrative domains within the DNS namespace, each containing resource records that define mappings between domain names and IP addresses. Common types of DNS records include A records (for IPv4 addresses), AAAA records (for IPv6 addresses), CNAME records (for aliasing), and MX records (for mail servers).

To create a new DNS zone using PowerShell, administrators can use the Add-DnsServerPrimaryZone cmdlet. For example:

sqlCopy code

```
Add-DnsServerPrimaryZone -Name "example.com" -ZoneFile "example.com.dns"
```

This command creates a new primary DNS zone for the domain "example.com" with a corresponding zone file.

Active Directory Integration: Active Directory relies heavily on DNS for locating domain controllers, domain services, and other AD-related resources. Active Directory-integrated DNS zones store DNS data in the AD database, providing benefits such as secure dynamic updates, replication via AD replication topology, and single-point management.

To integrate DNS with Active Directory during domain controller promotion, administrators can select the option to install DNS as part of the promotion process. Alternatively, they can manually configure DNS integration after promoting the domain controller.

Configuring DNS Forwarders: DNS forwarders are DNS servers that handle DNS queries on behalf of other DNS servers. They are typically used to forward external DNS queries to internet DNS servers when the local DNS server cannot resolve them directly.

To configure DNS forwarders using PowerShell, administrators can use the Set-DnsServerForwarder cmdlet. For example:

mathematicaCopy code

Set-DnsServerForwarder -IPAddress 8.8.8.8, 8.8.4.4

This command configures DNS forwarders to use Google's public DNS servers (8.8.8.8 and 8.8.4.4).

DNS Security Best Practices: DNS security is essential for protecting against various threats such as DNS spoofing, cache poisoning, and DDoS attacks. Best practices for DNS security include implementing DNSSEC (DNS Security Extensions), securing zone transfers, restricting zone transfers to authorized servers, and implementing DNS filtering solutions.

To enable DNSSEC for a DNS zone using PowerShell, administrators can use the Set-DnsServerZoneSigning cmdlet. For example:

sqlCopy code

Set-DnsServerZoneSigning -ZoneName "example.com" -Enable $true

This command enables DNSSEC for the "example.com" DNS zone.

Monitoring and Troubleshooting DNS: Monitoring and troubleshooting DNS involves tracking DNS query traffic, monitoring server performance, and diagnosing DNS-related issues. Tools such as DNS Manager, DNSLint, and nslookup can be used to analyze DNS configuration, troubleshoot DNS resolution problems, and verify DNS records.

Copy code

```
nslookup example.com
```

This command performs a DNS lookup for the domain "example.com" and returns the corresponding IP address.

DNS Load Balancing and Redundancy: DNS load balancing and redundancy techniques such as round-robin DNS and DNS failover help distribute client requests across multiple servers and ensure high availability of DNS services. These techniques improve service reliability and fault tolerance by distributing the load evenly and redirecting traffic in case of server failures.

To configure round-robin DNS for a domain using PowerShell, administrators can use the Add-DnsServerResourceRecordCName cmdlet to create multiple CNAME records pointing to different IP addresses.

In summary, DNS fundamentals and its integration with Active Directory are crucial aspects of network infrastructure in Windows environments. By understanding DNS principles, configuring DNS zones and records, integrating DNS with Active Directory, implementing security best practices, and leveraging monitoring and troubleshooting tools, administrators can ensure reliable and secure DNS services for their organizations.

Dynamic Host Configuration Protocol (DHCP) is a network protocol that automatically assigns IP addresses and other network configuration parameters to devices on a network. In Active Directory (AD) environments, DHCP plays a crucial role in simplifying IP address management and ensuring seamless connectivity for clients. This chapter delves into the setup and configuration of DHCP for Active Directory environments, covering essential concepts, best practices, and practical examples with CLI commands where applicable.

Understanding DHCP Fundamentals: DHCP automates the process of IP address allocation, allowing client devices to obtain IP addresses dynamically instead of relying on manual configuration. DHCP servers manage a pool of available IP addresses, lease durations, and other configuration options such as DNS server and default gateway settings.

Installing DHCP Server Role: In Windows Server environments, DHCP server functionality can be installed as a role using the Server Manager console or PowerShell commands.

mathematicaCopy code

```
Install-WindowsFeature -Name DHCP -IncludeManagementTools
```

This PowerShell command installs the DHCP Server role along with management tools on the current server.

Configuring DHCP Scopes: DHCP scopes define ranges of IP addresses that DHCP servers can allocate to clients. Administrators must configure DHCP scopes to match the subnetting scheme of their network and ensure that sufficient IP addresses are available to accommodate all clients.

To create a new DHCP scope using PowerShell, administrators can use the Add-DhcpServerv4Scope cmdlet. For example:

sqlCopy code

```
Add-DhcpServerv4Scope -Name "LAN" -StartRange 192.168.1.100 -EndRange 192.168.1.200 -SubnetMask 255.255.255.0 -LeaseDuration 8.0:0:0
```

This command creates a new DHCP scope named "LAN" with IP address range 192.168.1.100 to 192.168.1.200 and a lease duration of 8 days.

Configuring DHCP Options: DHCP options allow administrators to specify additional parameters such as DNS server addresses, default gateway, domain name, and WINS server settings to be provided to DHCP clients along with IP addresses.

To configure DHCP options using PowerShell, administrators can use the Set-DhcpServerv4OptionValue cmdlet. For example:

mathematicaCopy code

```
Set-DhcpServerv4OptionValue -OptionId 6 -Value "192.168.1.10, 192.168.1.11" -ScopeId "192.168.1.0"
```

This command sets the DNS server option (OptionId 6) to provide DNS server addresses 192.168.1.10 and 192.168.1.11 to clients in the specified DHCP scope.

DHCP Failover: DHCP failover provides redundancy and high availability for DHCP services by replicating DHCP lease information and configurations between two DHCP servers. In the event of a DHCP server failure, the standby server can take over lease management seamlessly.

To configure DHCP failover using PowerShell, administrators can use the Add-DhcpServerv4Failover cmdlet. For example:

mathematicaCopy code

```
Add-DhcpServerv4Failover -Name "DHCPFailover" -ScopeId "192.168.1.0" -PartnerServer "dhcp2.contoso.com" -Mode HotStandby
```

This command sets up DHCP failover between the current DHCP server and a partner server named "dhcp2.contoso.com" in hot standby mode.

DHCP Security Best Practices: DHCP security is essential for protecting against unauthorized access, rogue DHCP servers, and IP address conflicts. Best practices include securing DHCP server access, enabling DHCP snooping on network switches, and configuring DHCP server authentication.

To configure DHCP server authentication using PowerShell, administrators can use the Set-DhcpServerv4Filter cmdlet. For example:

mathematicaCopy code

```
Set-DhcpServerv4Filter -List Allow -MacAddress "00-15-5D-5D-64-7D"
```

This command allows a specific MAC address to bypass DHCP server packet filtering.

Monitoring and Troubleshooting DHCP: Monitoring and troubleshooting DHCP involve tracking DHCP lease information, monitoring server performance, and diagnosing DHCP-related issues such as IP address conflicts or lease exhaustion.

mathematicaCopy code

```
Get-DhcpServerv4Lease -ScopeId "192.168.1.0"
```

This command retrieves DHCP lease information for the specified DHCP scope.

DHCP Reservation: DHCP reservation allows administrators to assign a specific IP address to a client device based on its MAC address. This ensures that the device always receives the same IP address, making it easier to manage and troubleshoot.

To create a DHCP reservation using PowerShell, administrators can use the Add-DhcpServerv4Reservation cmdlet. For example:

arduinoCopy code

Add-DhcpServerv4Reservation -ScopeId "192.168.1.0" -IPAddress "192.168.1.150" -ClientId "00-15-5D-5D-64-7D" -Description "Printer"

This command creates a DHCP reservation for a printer with MAC address "00-15-5D-5D-64-7D" to always receive the IP address 192.168.1.150 within the specified DHCP scope.

In summary, DHCP setup and configuration are critical for providing automated IP address allocation and network configuration in Active Directory environments. By understanding DHCP fundamentals, configuring DHCP scopes and options, implementing failover and security measures, and leveraging monitoring and troubleshooting tools, administrators can ensure reliable and efficient DHCP services for their organizations.

Chapter 8: Active Directory Replication

Active Directory (AD) replication is a fundamental mechanism that ensures the consistency of directory data across domain controllers (DCs) within an AD forest. Replication topology defines the connections and communication paths between DCs, facilitating the efficient and timely exchange of directory updates. This chapter explores the intricacies of AD replication topology, including its components, design considerations, deployment techniques, and CLI commands for management.

Components of Replication Topology: AD replication topology comprises several key components:

Sites: Sites represent physical locations in the network and are defined based on network connectivity, such as subnets and network links. Each site contains one or more DCs responsible for servicing clients within that site.

Site Links: Site links define the connectivity between sites and determine the replication schedule and transport method (e.g., RPC or SMTP) for replication traffic.

Bridgehead Servers: Bridgehead servers are designated DCs responsible for managing replication traffic between sites. They serve as entry points for replication data flowing in and out of their respective sites.

Design Considerations: Designing an effective replication topology requires careful consideration of various factors:

Network Topology: Understanding the organization's network infrastructure, including WAN links, bandwidth, latency, and reliability, is essential for designing an optimal replication topology.

Site Boundaries: Creating site boundaries based on geographic locations, network segments, or administrative boundaries helps optimize replication traffic and minimize network congestion.

Replication Schedule: Configuring replication schedules based on network usage patterns and business requirements ensures timely replication without overwhelming network resources.

Deploying Replication Topology: Deploying an AD replication topology involves several steps:

Creating Sites: Use the Active Directory Sites and Services console (dssite.msc) or PowerShell commands to create sites corresponding to physical locations.

sqlCopy code

```
New-ADReplicationSite -Name "Site1"
```

Defining Subnets: Associate subnets with sites to facilitate client authentication and optimize replication traffic routing.

sqlCopy code

```
New-ADReplicationSubnet -Name "192.168.1.0/24" -Site "Site1"
```

Configuring Site Links: Create site links to define connectivity between sites and specify replication schedules and transport methods.

sqlCopy code

```
New-ADReplicationSiteLink -Name "SiteLink1" -SitesIncluded "Site1","Site2" -ReplicationFrequency 15 -ReplicationInterval 180
```

Managing Replication Topology: Once deployed, AD replication topology requires ongoing management to ensure its effectiveness:

Monitoring Replication Status: Use tools like repadmin.exe or PowerShell cmdlets to monitor replication status, detect replication failures, and troubleshoot issues.

bashCopy code

repadmin /replsummary

Forcing Replication: In scenarios where immediate replication is required, administrators can force replication between specific DCs using CLI commands.

bashCopy code

```
repadmin /syncall /A /P /e
```

Optimizing Replication Traffic: Adjusting replication schedules, modifying site link costs, or deploying additional bridgehead servers can help optimize replication traffic and improve overall performance.

Site Link Bridging and Optimization: Site link bridging enables transitive replication between sites, allowing changes made in one site to propagate to other sites through intermediary sites. This feature helps optimize replication traffic and reduce the need for direct connections between all sites.

Handling Intersite Replication Issues: Intersite replication issues may arise due to network connectivity problems, bandwidth limitations, or configuration errors. Troubleshooting such issues requires thorough analysis of replication logs, network traces, and DC health status.

Replication Topology Best Practices: Adhering to best practices ensures a robust and efficient replication topology:

Regular Monitoring: Continuously monitor replication status and address any anomalies promptly to maintain AD health.

Testing Changes: Before making significant changes to the replication topology, conduct thorough testing in a lab environment to assess the impact on production AD.

Documenting Configurations: Documenting replication topology configurations, including site designs, site links, and bridgehead servers, helps maintain visibility and facilitates troubleshooting.

Future Trends and Technologies: Emerging technologies such as Active Directory Federation Services (AD FS) and Azure AD Connect introduce new replication requirements and considerations. Understanding these trends is crucial for designing scalable and future-proof replication topologies.

In summary, understanding Active Directory replication topology is essential for maintaining a healthy and resilient AD infrastructure. By considering design principles, deploying appropriate configurations, and employing effective management practices, administrators can ensure reliable replication and optimal performance across their AD environments.

Active Directory (AD) replication is a critical process that ensures the consistency and integrity of directory data across domain controllers (DCs) within an AD forest. However, replication issues can occur due to various factors, such as network problems, configuration errors, or DC hardware failures. Monitoring and troubleshooting replication issues are essential tasks for maintaining a healthy AD environment. This chapter explores the techniques, tools, and best practices for monitoring and troubleshooting replication issues, including practical examples and CLI commands for effective management.

Understanding Replication Monitoring: Replication monitoring involves tracking the replication status and health of AD replication links, ensuring that changes made on one DC are propagated to other DCs in a timely manner. Monitoring replication is crucial for identifying and resolving issues before they impact AD operations.

Replication Monitoring Tools: Several tools are available for monitoring AD replication, including built-in utilities and third-party solutions:

repadmin.exe: Repadmin is a command-line tool provided by Microsoft for monitoring and managing AD replication. It offers various commands for checking replication status, forcing replication, and diagnosing replication problems.

bashCopy code

repadmin /showrepl

This command displays the replication status of all DCs in the forest.

Active Directory Replication Status Tool (ADREPLSTATUS): ADREPLSTATUS is a graphical tool that provides detailed replication status information for DCs in an AD forest. It allows administrators to view replication errors, latency, and topology information in an easy-to-understand format.

Event Viewer: The Event Viewer console can be used to view AD-related event logs, including replication events. Replication-related errors and warnings are logged in the Directory Service event log, providing valuable insights into replication issues.

Common Replication Issues: Replication issues can manifest in various forms, each requiring different troubleshooting approaches:

Replication Latency: High replication latency indicates delays in replicating changes between DCs, which can lead to data inconsistency and authentication problems for clients.

Replication Errors: Replication errors such as "Access Denied" or "RPC Server Unavailable" signify communication or permission issues between DCs.

USN Rollback: USN rollback occurs when a DC receives updates from another DC with a lower Update Sequence Number (USN), leading to data corruption and replication conflicts.

Troubleshooting Replication Issues: Troubleshooting replication issues involves a systematic approach to identify and resolve underlying problems:

Reviewing Replication Status: Start by using tools like repadmin.exe or ADREPLSTATUS to check the replication status of DCs and identify any replication errors or warnings.

Analyzing Replication Metadata: Use the repadmin.exe command-line tool to query replication metadata and identify the source of replication failures.

phpCopy code

```
repadmin /showmetadata <DCName> <ObjectDN>
```

Checking Network Connectivity: Verify network connectivity between DCs using tools like ping or tracert to ensure that replication traffic can traverse the network without issues.

Examining Firewall Settings: Firewall misconfigurations can block replication traffic between DCs. Ensure that necessary ports (e.g., TCP 389, TCP 636) are open on firewalls between DCs.

Inspecting DNS Configuration: Incorrect DNS settings can prevent DCs from locating each other for replication. Verify DNS resolution and ensure that DCs are correctly registered in DNS.

Forcing Replication: In cases where replication is delayed or stalled, administrators can force replication between specific DCs to synchronize directory changes manually.

bashCopy code

```
repadmin /syncall /A /P /d /e
```

Resolving Replication Errors: Address replication errors based on their root causes, such as network issues, AD object permissions, or DC hardware failures.

Best Practices for Replication Monitoring and Troubleshooting: Adhering to best practices ensures effective replication monitoring and troubleshooting:

Regular Monitoring: Implement a regular monitoring routine to detect replication issues early and prevent data inconsistencies.

Documenting Changes: Document any changes made to AD replication topology or configuration settings to facilitate troubleshooting efforts.

Testing Procedures: Test replication troubleshooting procedures in a controlled environment to validate their effectiveness before applying them in production.

Keeping Systems Updated: Ensure that DCs are running the latest Windows updates and patches to address known replication-related issues and vulnerabilities.

Automating Monitoring and Alerting: Automate replication monitoring and alerting processes using PowerShell scripts or third-party monitoring solutions to proactively identify and address replication issues.

Collaborating with Support: In complex or persistent replication issues, collaborate with Microsoft support or knowledgeable peers to leverage their expertise and resources for resolution.

In summary, monitoring and troubleshooting replication issues are critical tasks for maintaining a healthy and reliable Active Directory environment. By employing the right tools, following best practices, and leveraging systematic troubleshooting approaches, administrators can effectively identify, diagnose, and resolve replication issues, ensuring the integrity and consistency of directory data across the AD forest.

Chapter 9: Backup and Disaster Recovery Strategies

Active Directory (AD) is a critical component of most enterprise IT environments, serving as the central repository for user accounts, group policies, authentication, and access control information. Any disruption or loss of AD data can have severe consequences for an organization, leading to downtime, data loss, and security breaches. Therefore, implementing robust backup strategies is essential to safeguard AD data and ensure business continuity. This chapter explores best practices for Active Directory backup, including backup types, frequency, storage considerations, recovery strategies, and practical examples with CLI commands where applicable.

Understanding Active Directory Backup: Active Directory backup involves creating copies of AD data, including the AD database (NTDS.dit), SYSVOL folder, and registry settings. Backups serve as a safeguard against accidental deletions, hardware failures, software bugs, and malicious attacks that could compromise AD integrity.

Backup Types: There are several types of backups that administrators can perform in Active Directory:

Full Backup: A full backup includes all AD data, including the AD database, SYSVOL, and registry settings. It provides the most comprehensive protection but may require significant storage space and time to complete.

Incremental Backup: An incremental backup captures only the changes made since the last backup, reducing backup size and duration. However, restoring from incremental backups may require multiple backup sets.

Differential Backup: A differential backup captures all changes made since the last full backup. Unlike incremental backups, restoring from a differential backup only requires the last full backup and the most recent differential backup.

Backup Frequency: Determining the backup frequency depends on various factors, including business requirements, data sensitivity, and recovery objectives:

Daily Backups: Performing daily backups ensures that recent changes are captured regularly, minimizing data loss in the event of a failure.

Regular Full Backups: Regular full backups, combined with periodic incremental or differential backups, provide a balance between data protection and storage efficiency.

Storage Considerations: Choosing the right storage solution for AD backups is crucial for ensuring data integrity, accessibility, and scalability:

Offsite Backup Storage: Storing backups offsite protects against localized disasters such as fires, floods, or theft. Cloud-based storage solutions or remote data centers are ideal for offsite backup storage.

Redundant Storage: Implementing redundant storage mechanisms such as RAID arrays, mirrored drives, or geographically dispersed backups enhances data availability and resilience.

Backup and Restore Procedures: Developing comprehensive backup and restore procedures ensures that AD data can be recovered quickly and efficiently in the event of a disaster:

Backup Automation: Automate backup processes using PowerShell scripts or third-party backup solutions to minimize manual intervention and ensure consistency.

Regular Testing: Regularly test backup and restore procedures in a controlled environment to validate their effectiveness and identify any potential issues.

Retention Policies: Establish retention policies to manage backup retention periods, archival practices, and data lifecycle management.

Backup CLI Commands: In Windows Server environments, administrators can perform AD backups using various CLI commands and PowerShell cmdlets:

ntdsutil.exe: The ntdsutil command-line utility provides options for backing up and restoring the AD database.
arduinoCopy code

```
ntdsutil.exe "activate instance ntds" "ifm" "create sysvol full c:\backup" q q
```

Windows Server Backup (wbadmin): The wbadmin command-line tool allows administrators to perform system state backups, including AD data.
mathematicaCopy code

```
wbadmin start systemstatebackup -backupTarget:D:
```

Disaster Recovery Strategies: In addition to regular backups, organizations should develop disaster recovery strategies to minimize downtime and data loss during AD recovery:

Backup Rotation: Implementing backup rotation schemes such as Grandfather-Father-Son (GFS) or Tower of Hanoi ensures that multiple backup sets are retained at different intervals.

Emergency Recovery Procedures: Document emergency recovery procedures to guide administrators through the process of restoring AD data in critical situations.

Monitoring and Auditing: Monitoring backup jobs and auditing backup logs are essential for ensuring backup success and identifying any issues or failures:

Event Log Monitoring: Regularly review event logs for backup-related events, errors, or warnings that may indicate problems with the backup process.

Alerting Mechanisms: Implement alerting mechanisms to notify administrators of backup failures or anomalies, enabling prompt action and resolution.

In summary, implementing effective Active Directory backup best practices is crucial for protecting AD data and ensuring business continuity. By understanding backup types, frequency, storage considerations, and recovery strategies, administrators can develop robust backup strategies that meet organizational requirements and mitigate the risk of data loss or downtime in the event of a disaster.

Disasters, whether they are natural or human-made, can strike at any time and have the potential to disrupt business operations significantly. For organizations relying on Active Directory (AD) for their identity and access management, having a robust disaster recovery plan in place is essential to minimize downtime, data loss, and ensure business continuity. This chapter explores the importance of disaster recovery planning for Active Directory environments, key components of a disaster recovery plan, best practices for disaster recovery procedures, and practical examples with CLI commands where applicable.

Importance of Disaster Recovery Planning: Disaster recovery planning is crucial for organizations to mitigate the impact of unexpected events and ensure the resilience of their IT infrastructure. In the context of Active Directory, a comprehensive disaster recovery plan helps organizations recover AD services and data quickly, minimizing the impact on business operations and maintaining regulatory compliance.

Components of a Disaster Recovery Plan: A well-designed disaster recovery plan for Active Directory should include the following components:

Risk Assessment: Conduct a thorough risk assessment to identify potential threats, vulnerabilities, and the potential impact of disasters on AD services and data.

Business Impact Analysis (BIA): Perform a BIA to prioritize AD components and services based on their criticality to business operations. This helps allocate resources and prioritize recovery efforts accordingly.

Backup and Restore Procedures: Define backup strategies, including backup frequency, retention policies, and storage mechanisms for AD data. Establish procedures for restoring AD services and data from backups in the event of a disaster.

Disaster Recovery Team: Formulate a dedicated disaster recovery team responsible for executing the disaster recovery plan, coordinating recovery efforts, and communicating with stakeholders during emergencies.

Communication Plan: Develop a communication plan to ensure timely and accurate dissemination of information to employees, customers, partners, and other stakeholders during a disaster.

Testing and Training: Regularly test the disaster recovery plan through tabletop exercises, simulations, or full-scale drills to identify gaps, validate procedures, and familiarize personnel with their roles and responsibilities.

Backup and Restore Procedures: Backup and restore procedures are integral to Active Directory disaster recovery. Organizations should implement the following best practices:

Regular Backups: Perform regular backups of AD data, including the AD database (NTDS.dit), SYSVOL, and system state, using tools such as Windows Server Backup (wbadmin) or third-party backup solutions.

mathematicaCopy code

wbadmin start systemstatebackup -backupTarget:D:

Offsite Storage: Store backup copies of AD data offsite to protect against localized disasters such as fires, floods, or theft. Cloud-based storage solutions or remote data centers are ideal for offsite backup storage.

Backup Encryption: Encrypt backup data to protect sensitive AD information from unauthorized access or disclosure. Use built-in encryption features or third-party encryption solutions to secure backup files.

Backup Validation: Regularly validate backup integrity and perform test restores to ensure that backups are complete, consistent, and recoverable in the event of a disaster.

Disaster Recovery CLI Commands: In Windows Server environments, administrators can perform various disaster recovery tasks using CLI commands and PowerShell cmdlets:

Active Directory Recycle Bin: Enable the Active Directory Recycle Bin feature to facilitate the recovery of deleted AD objects without resorting to authoritative restores.

sqlCopy code

```
Enable-ADOptionalFeature  -Identity  'Recycle  Bin
Feature'  -Scope  ForestOrConfigurationSet  -Target
'<DomainController>'
```

Authoritative Restore: Perform an authoritative restore of AD objects using the ntdsutil command-line utility to recover deleted or modified objects from backup.

arduinoCopy code

```
ntdsutil.exe  "authoritative  restore"  "restore  object
<ObjectDN>"
```

Non-Authoritative Restore: Perform a non-authoritative restore of AD data using Windows Server Backup to restore AD data from a backup without marking it as authoritative.

phpCopy code

```
wbadmin        start        systemstaterecovery        -
version:<BackupVersion>
```

Testing and Training: Regular testing and training are essential to ensure the effectiveness of the disaster recovery plan:

Tabletop Exercises: Conduct tabletop exercises to simulate various disaster scenarios, assess the response capabilities of the disaster recovery team, and identify areas for improvement.

Drills and Simulations: Perform full-scale disaster recovery drills and simulations to test the execution of recovery procedures, validate recovery time objectives (RTOs) and recovery point objectives (RPOs), and evaluate the overall effectiveness of the plan.

Continuous Improvement: Disaster recovery planning is an ongoing process that requires regular review, updates, and improvements:

Post-Incident Review: Conduct post-incident reviews following actual disasters or simulated exercises to identify lessons learned, document successes and challenges, and update the disaster recovery plan accordingly.

Incident Response Plan: Integrate the disaster recovery plan with the organization's broader incident response plan to ensure a coordinated and effective response to emergencies.

Documentation and Documentation: Document all aspects of the disaster recovery plan, including procedures, responsibilities, contact information, and recovery strategies, in a comprehensive and easily accessible format.

In summary, disaster recovery planning and procedures are essential for ensuring the resilience and continuity of Active Directory services and data in the face of unexpected events. By implementing a comprehensive disaster recovery plan, defining backup and restore procedures, conducting regular testing and training, and continuously improving the plan based on lessons learned, organizations can minimize the impact of disasters and maintain business operations even in challenging circumstances.

Chapter 10: Troubleshooting Common Active Directory Issues

Login and authentication are fundamental processes in any IT infrastructure, including Active Directory (AD) environments. Users rely on these processes to access resources, applications, and services securely. However, various factors can lead to login and authentication problems, causing frustration for users and administrators alike. This chapter explores some of the most common login and authentication problems in AD environments, their underlying causes, troubleshooting techniques, and practical examples with CLI commands where applicable.

Incorrect Credentials: One of the most prevalent login problems is users entering incorrect credentials. This could be due to typos, forgotten passwords, or expired credentials. To troubleshoot this issue:

Verify Credentials: Ensure that users are entering the correct username and password. If necessary, reset the user's password using the following CLI command:

phpCopy code

```
net user <username> <newpassword>
```

Check Password Expiry: Determine if the user's password has expired and prompt them to reset it. Administrators can enforce password policies to require regular password changes.

Account Lockouts: Account lockouts occur when users exceed the maximum number of failed login attempts, triggering a security measure to protect against brute-force attacks. To address account lockouts:

Unlock Account: Unlock the user's account using the following CLI command:

bashCopy code

```
net user <username> /active:yes
```

Investigate Root Cause: Investigate the source of repeated login failures, which could be due to forgotten passwords, automated scripts, or malicious activity.

Expired Accounts: Users may experience login failures if their accounts are expired or disabled. To address this issue:

Enable Account: Enable the user's account if it has been disabled using the following CLI command:

bashCopy code

```
net user <username> /active:yes
```

Review Account Expiry: Monitor account expiration dates and proactively renew or extend account validity as needed.

Network Connectivity Issues: Network connectivity problems can prevent users from accessing AD authentication services, leading to login failures. To troubleshoot network connectivity issues:

Ping Test: Use the ping command to test connectivity between the client device and the domain controller:

phpCopy code

```
ping <domaincontroller>
```

Check DNS Resolution: Ensure that DNS resolution is functioning correctly, as AD authentication relies heavily on DNS. Use the nslookup command to verify DNS resolution:

phpCopy code

```
nslookup <domaincontroller>
```

Time Synchronization Problems: Inconsistent time settings between client devices and domain controllers can cause authentication failures due to Kerberos ticket issues. To address time synchronization problems:

Check Time Settings: Verify that the time settings are synchronized between client devices and domain controllers. Use the following CLI command to synchronize time with a domain controller:

```bash
bashCopy code
w32tm /resync /rediscover
```

Configure Time Service: Ensure that the Windows Time service (W32Time) is running and configured correctly on all domain controllers and client devices.

Trust Relationship Failures: Trust relationship failures occur when the secure channel between a client device and the domain is broken. This can happen due to various reasons, such as machine account password mismatches or Active Directory issues. To address trust relationship failures:

Reset Computer Account: Reset the computer account of the affected client device using the following CLI command:

```bash
bashCopy code
netdom        resetpwd        /s:<domaincontroller>
/ud:<domain>\<username> /pd:*
```

Rejoin Domain: If resetting the computer account does not resolve the issue, disjoin the client device from the domain and rejoin it.

Certificate Issues: Certificate-related problems can prevent users from authenticating to AD-secured services, such as websites or VPNs. To troubleshoot certificate issues:

Check Certificate Validity: Verify that the SSL/TLS certificate used by the AD-secured service is valid and has not expired.

Review Certificate Trust Chains: Ensure that the client device trusts the certificate authority (CA) that issued the server's certificate.

Group Policy Problems: Group Policy misconfigurations can affect user authentication and access control settings, leading to login problems. To troubleshoot Group Policy problems:

Group Policy Results: Use the gpresult command to check the applied Group Policy settings on the client device:

```bash
bashCopy code
```

gpresult /r

Event Viewer: Review the Event Viewer logs on the client device and domain controllers for Group Policy-related errors or warnings.

In summary, common login and authentication problems in Active Directory environments can stem from a variety of causes, including incorrect credentials, account lockouts, network connectivity issues, time synchronization problems, trust relationship failures, certificate issues, and Group Policy problems. By understanding the underlying causes of these problems and using appropriate troubleshooting techniques, administrators can resolve login issues efficiently, minimize user downtime, and ensure the security and integrity of their AD environment.

Group Policy is a powerful tool in Active Directory (AD) environments, allowing administrators to centrally manage and enforce configurations, settings, and security policies across multiple computers and users. However, Group Policy application failures can occur, resulting in inconsistencies in configuration settings, security vulnerabilities, and user experience issues. This chapter explores the common causes of Group Policy application failures, troubleshooting techniques, and best practices for resolving issues, including practical examples with CLI commands where applicable.

Introduction to Group Policy Application Failures: Group Policy application failures occur when Group Policy settings do not apply as intended to target computers or users. These failures can lead to inconsistencies in configuration settings, security vulnerabilities, and user experience issues. Understanding the common causes of Group Policy application failures is essential for effective troubleshooting and resolution.

Common Causes of Group Policy Application Failures:
Group Policy application failures can be attributed to various factors, including:

Network Connectivity Issues: Network connectivity problems between client computers and domain controllers can prevent Group Policy from being applied successfully.

Permissions Issues: Insufficient permissions or misconfigured security settings can prevent Group Policy from being read or applied by target computers or users.

Replication Problems: Inconsistent replication between domain controllers can lead to discrepancies in Group Policy settings, causing application failures on some computers or users.

Registry or File System Corruption: Corruption in the registry or file system of target computers can prevent Group Policy from being processed correctly.

WMI Repository Corruption: Corruption in the Windows Management Instrumentation (WMI) repository can affect Group Policy processing, leading to application failures.

Troubleshooting Group Policy Application Failures:
Troubleshooting Group Policy application failures involves a systematic approach to identify and resolve underlying issues:

Verify Group Policy Scope: Use the Group Policy Management Console (GPMC) to verify the scope of Group Policy settings and ensure that they apply to the correct organizational units (OUs), domains, or sites.

Review Group Policy Events: Review Event Viewer logs on target computers and domain controllers for Group Policy-related events, errors, or warnings. Look for Event IDs such as 1058 (Group Policy processing failed) and 7016 (Completed Group Policy processing).

Check Group Policy Modeling and Results: Use the Group Policy Modeling and Group Policy Results wizards in GPMC to simulate Group Policy application and identify any issues or conflicts.

Test Group Policy on Individual Computers: Apply Group Policy settings to individual computers or users using the gpupdate command-line tool to isolate issues and test potential solutions.

bashCopy code

gpupdate /force

Use RSOP and GPResult: Use the Resultant Set of Policy (RSOP) and gpresult command-line tools to diagnose Group Policy settings applied to target computers or users.

bashCopy code

gpresult /r

Resolve Group Policy Application Failures: Once the root cause of Group Policy application failures is identified, take appropriate action to resolve the issue:

Address Network Connectivity Issues: Troubleshoot network connectivity problems between client computers and domain controllers by checking DNS resolution, firewall settings, and network hardware.

Resolve Permissions Issues: Ensure that target computers and users have the necessary permissions to read and apply Group Policy settings. Use tools like the Effective Permissions feature in Active Directory Users and Computers to troubleshoot permissions issues.

Fix Replication Problems: Resolve replication inconsistencies between domain controllers by verifying replication topology, forcing replication between domain controllers, and monitoring replication status using tools like repadmin.

bashCopy code

repadmin /showrepl

Repair Registry or File System Corruption: Use built-in Windows utilities like System File Checker (sfc) and Deployment Image Servicing and Management (DISM) to repair corrupted system files and registry settings on target computers.

Rebuild WMI Repository: Rebuild the WMI repository on target computers experiencing Group Policy application failures using the following CLI commands:

bashCopy code

```
winmgmt /verifyrepository winmgmt /salvagerepository
```

Best Practices for Preventing Group Policy Application Failures: Implementing best practices can help prevent Group Policy application failures and ensure smooth operations in AD environments:

Regular Monitoring and Maintenance: Monitor Group Policy processing, event logs, and replication status regularly to detect and address issues proactively.

Standardize Group Policy Settings: Standardize Group Policy settings across the organization to reduce complexity and minimize the risk of conflicts or inconsistencies.

Document Changes: Document any changes made to Group Policy settings, including modifications, additions, or deletions, to facilitate troubleshooting and auditing.

Test Changes in a Lab Environment: Test changes to Group Policy settings in a lab environment before deploying them in production to identify potential conflicts or issues.

Training and Education: Provide training and education to IT staff and end-users on Group Policy best practices, troubleshooting techniques, and potential pitfalls to minimize user errors and improve overall system reliability.

In summary, Group Policy application failures can occur due to various factors, including network connectivity issues, permissions problems, replication inconsistencies, registry or file system corruption, and WMI repository errors. By understanding the common causes of Group Policy application failures and following best practices for troubleshooting and resolution, administrators can ensure the smooth and reliable application of Group Policy settings in Active Directory environments, minimizing disruptions and enhancing overall system stability and security.

BOOK 2
MASTERING ACTIVE DIRECTORY
ADVANCED TECHNIQUES FOR SYSTEM ADMINISTRATORS

ROB BOTWRIGHT

Chapter 1: Advanced Active Directory Infrastructure Design

Multi-domain and multi-forest architectures are common in large-scale enterprise environments where organizational structure, geographical distribution, or security requirements necessitate the segmentation of Active Directory (AD) resources. These architectures provide flexibility, scalability, and isolation, but they also introduce complexity in design, implementation, and management. This chapter explores the principles, considerations, best practices, and practical examples for designing multi-domain and multi-forest architectures, including CLI commands where applicable.

Introduction to Multi-Domain and Multi-Forest Architectures: Multi-domain and multi-forest architectures involve the deployment of multiple AD domains or forests within an organization. Domains and forests serve as administrative and security boundaries, allowing organizations to segregate resources, delegate administrative control, and enforce security policies as needed.

Principles of Multi-Domain and Multi-Forest Architectures: Understanding the principles underlying multi-domain and multi-forest architectures is essential for effective design:

Administrative Boundary: Domains and forests serve as administrative boundaries, enabling organizations to delegate administrative control and responsibilities to specific groups or departments.

Security Isolation: Segregating resources into separate domains or forests allows organizations to enforce security policies and access controls tailored to specific business units, projects, or geographical locations.

82

Resource Segmentation: Multi-domain and multi-forest architectures enable organizations to segment resources based on factors such as data sensitivity, regulatory compliance requirements, or operational needs.

Considerations for Designing Multi-Domain and Multi-Forest Architectures: When designing multi-domain and multi-forest architectures, several considerations must be taken into account:

Organizational Structure: Align the domain and forest structure with the organization's hierarchy, business units, geographical locations, and administrative boundaries.

Trust Relationships: Establish trust relationships between domains or forests to facilitate resource sharing, authentication, and access across administrative boundaries.

Resource Access Requirements: Analyze resource access requirements to determine the appropriate level of isolation and segmentation needed for different types of resources.

Replication Topology: Design an efficient replication topology to ensure timely and reliable replication between domain controllers within and across domains or forests.

Security Policies: Define and enforce security policies consistently across domains or forests to maintain security posture and compliance with regulatory requirements.

Best Practices for Designing Multi-Domain and Multi-Forest Architectures: Implementing best practices can help streamline the design, implementation, and management of multi-domain and multi-forest architectures:

Simplify Where Possible: Minimize complexity by consolidating domains or forests where feasible, leveraging organizational units (OUs) and group-based access controls for finer-grained control.

Use Transitive Trusts: Establish transitive trust relationships between domains or forests to simplify resource access and authentication across administrative boundaries.

Centralize Administration: Centralize administration where possible to reduce administrative overhead and ensure consistency in policy enforcement and management practices.

Plan for Growth: Design the architecture with scalability in mind to accommodate future growth, mergers, acquisitions, or restructuring initiatives.

Document Design Decisions: Document the rationale behind design decisions, including domain and forest structure, trust relationships, replication topology, and security policies, to facilitate understanding and future updates.

Practical Examples and CLI Commands: Implementing multi-domain and multi-forest architectures involves various tasks and CLI commands:

Creating Domains and Forests: Use the dcpromo command-line tool to promote servers to domain controllers and create new domains or forests.

bashCopy code

```
dcpromo /unattend /replicaOrNewDomain:domain
/newDomain:forest /newDomainDnsName:<domainname>
/domainNetBiosName:<NetBiosName>
/forestLevel:<forestlevel> /domainLevel:<domainlevel>
/safeModeAdminPassword:<password>
```

Establishing Trust Relationships: Use the Netdom command-line tool to create trust relationships between domains or forests.

bashCopy code

```
netdom trust <trustedDomain> /domain:<trustedDomain>
/add
```

Managing Replication: Use the repadmin command-line tool to monitor and manage replication between domain controllers.

bashCopy code

repadmin /syncall /A /e

Challenges and Considerations: While multi-domain and multi-forest architectures offer numerous benefits, they also present challenges:

Increased Complexity: Managing multiple domains or forests adds complexity to administration, troubleshooting, and security management.

Resource Redundancy: Duplication of resources and administrative effort may occur across domains or forests, leading to inefficiencies and increased operational overhead.

Inter-Domain or Inter-Forest Communication: Ensuring seamless communication and interoperability between domains or forests requires careful planning and configuration of trust relationships, DNS resolution, and network connectivity.

Monitoring and Maintenance: Regular monitoring and maintenance are essential for ensuring the stability, performance, and security of multi-domain and multi-forest architectures:

Active Directory Health Checks: Perform regular health checks of Active Directory components, including domain controllers, replication status, trust relationships, and security policies.

Security Audits: Conduct periodic security audits to identify vulnerabilities, misconfigurations, or unauthorized access across domains or forests.

Performance Optimization: Monitor performance metrics such as CPU utilization, memory usage, and disk I/O to identify and address performance bottlenecks in multi-domain and multi-forest environments.

In summary, designing multi-domain and multi-forest architectures requires careful consideration of organizational structure, resource access requirements, security policies, and scalability needs. By following best practices, leveraging CLI commands for implementation tasks, and addressing challenges proactively, organizations can build robust, flexible, and secure Active Directory environments that meet the needs of their business operations.

Active Directory (AD) trust relationships play a pivotal role in enabling seamless resource access and authentication across domains or forests within an organization. Trust relationships establish a secure communication channel between domains or forests, allowing users, groups, and computers to interact transparently across administrative boundaries. This chapter delves into the significance of trust relationships, their types, implementation considerations, best practices, and practical examples with CLI commands where applicable.

Understanding Active Directory Trust Relationships: Active Directory trust relationships define the level of trust and security between two domains or forests. They enable users in one domain or forest to access resources in another domain or forest while maintaining security boundaries. Trust relationships authenticate users, groups, and computers across administrative boundaries, facilitating resource sharing and collaboration.

Types of Trust Relationships: Active Directory supports various types of trust relationships, each serving specific use cases and requirements:

One-Way Trust: In a one-way trust, Domain A trusts Domain B, allowing users in Domain B to access resources in Domain

A. However, users in Domain A cannot access resources in Domain B unless a separate trust is established.

Two-Way Trust: In a two-way trust, Domain A trusts Domain B, and Domain B trusts Domain A. This bidirectional trust enables users in both domains to access resources in each other's domains.

Transitive Trust: Transitive trusts enable indirect trust relationships between multiple domains within a forest. If Domain A trusts Domain B and Domain B trusts Domain C, then Domain A trusts Domain C implicitly.

External Trust: External trusts establish trust relationships between domains in separate forests or non-AD LDAP directories. External trusts are often used in scenarios involving mergers, acquisitions, or partnerships between organizations with separate AD infrastructures.

Considerations for Implementing Trust Relationships: Implementing trust relationships requires careful planning and consideration of various factors:

Security Requirements: Determine the level of trust and security required between domains or forests based on organizational policies, compliance requirements, and risk tolerance.

Administrative Boundaries: Align trust relationships with administrative boundaries, business units, and resource access requirements to ensure appropriate access controls and segregation of duties.

Authentication Mechanisms: Choose the appropriate authentication mechanism for trust relationships, such as Kerberos or NTLM, based on security requirements and compatibility between domains or forests.

Transitivity: Decide whether to enable transitive trusts to facilitate indirect trust relationships between multiple domains within a forest or to limit trust relationships to specific domains or forests for tighter security controls.

Implementing Trust Relationships: Implementing trust relationships involves several steps, including establishing trust, configuring trust properties, and validating trust functionality:

Establishing Trust: Use the Active Directory Domains and Trusts console or the Netdom command-line tool to establish trust relationships between domains or forests.

bashCopy code

```
netdom trust <trustedDomain> /domain:<trustedDomain> /add
```

Configuring Trust Properties: Configure trust properties, such as trust type (one-way or two-way), transitivity, authentication mechanisms, and selective authentication, to align with security and access requirements.

Validating Trust Functionality: Validate trust functionality by accessing resources in the trusted domain or forest using credentials from the trusting domain or forest. Use tools like the NLTest command-line tool to verify trust status and domain controller connectivity.

bashCopy code

```
nltest /dsgetdc:<trustedDomain>
```

Best Practices for Implementing Trust Relationships: Following best practices can help ensure the successful implementation and management of trust relationships:

Limit Trust Scope: Limit the scope of trust relationships to specific domains or forests and avoid establishing overly permissive trusts to minimize the risk of unauthorized access and security breaches.

Regular Monitoring: Monitor trust relationships regularly for changes, anomalies, or security incidents using tools like the Active Directory Replication Status Tool (ADREPLSTATUS) or PowerShell scripts.

Documentation and Auditing: Document trust relationships, including trust properties, authentication mechanisms, and trust validation procedures, to facilitate auditing, troubleshooting, and compliance with regulatory requirements.

Trust Validation: Validate trust functionality periodically to ensure that trust relationships are functioning as expected and that users can access resources across trusted domains or forests seamlessly.

Challenges and Considerations: Implementing and managing trust relationships may present challenges and considerations:

Security Risks: Inappropriate trust configurations or mismanagement of trust relationships can expose organizations to security risks, such as unauthorized access, data leakage, or lateral movement by attackers.

Complexity: Managing trust relationships in large, complex AD environments with multiple domains or forests requires careful planning, coordination, and ongoing maintenance to ensure consistency and security.

Impact on Authentication: Changes to trust relationships, such as adding or removing trusts, can impact user authentication, resource access, and group membership, requiring careful coordination and communication with stakeholders.

Case Study: Implementing Trust Relationships: Consider a scenario where two organizations merge, each with its own AD infrastructure. To enable seamless resource access and collaboration between the merged organizations, administrators establish a two-way trust relationship between the domains, configure trust properties, validate trust functionality, and monitor trust status regularly to ensure security and compliance.

In summary, implementing Active Directory trust relationships is essential for enabling secure resource access and authentication across domains or forests within an organization. By understanding the types of trust relationships, considering implementation factors, following best practices, and leveraging CLI commands for trust configuration and validation, administrators can establish robust trust relationships that support organizational goals, security requirements, and regulatory compliance.

Chapter 2: Implementing Active Directory Federation Services (AD FS)

Single Sign-On (SSO) is a crucial component of modern identity and access management solutions, enabling users to access multiple applications and services with a single set of credentials. Active Directory Federation Services (AD FS) is Microsoft's solution for implementing SSO across different platforms and applications, both within and outside an organization's network boundaries. This chapter explores the significance of SSO, the role of AD FS, considerations for configuration, best practices, and practical examples with CLI commands where applicable.

Understanding Single Sign-On (SSO): Single Sign-On (SSO) allows users to authenticate once and gain access to multiple applications or services without needing to re-enter credentials. SSO enhances user experience, improves productivity, and reduces the burden on users to remember multiple passwords for different systems.

Role of Active Directory Federation Services (AD FS): AD FS is a component of the Windows Server operating system that provides SSO capabilities by federating authentication between trusted identity providers and relying parties. AD FS acts as a federation service, enabling users to use their corporate credentials to access external resources securely.

Considerations for Configuring AD FS for SSO: Configuring AD FS for SSO requires careful planning and consideration of various factors:

Identity Providers: Determine the identity providers that will authenticate users for SSO, such as Active Directory, Azure Active Directory, or third-party identity providers.

Relying Parties: Identify the applications or services that will trust AD FS for authentication (relying parties) and ensure they are compatible with SAML (Security Assertion Markup Language) or WS-Federation protocols.

Certificate Management: Configure and manage certificates for securing communication between AD FS servers, relying parties, and clients. Certificates are essential for encrypting and signing SAML tokens used in SSO transactions.

Configuring AD FS for SSO: Configuring AD FS for SSO involves several steps, including setting up AD FS servers, configuring trust relationships, and enabling SSO for relying parties:

Install AD FS Role: Install the AD FS role on Windows Server using the Server Manager or PowerShell commands.

sqlCopy code

```
Add-WindowsFeature ADFS-Federation
```

Configure AD FS Farm: Set up an AD FS farm with multiple servers for high availability and fault tolerance. Configure the AD FS service properties, including federation service name, SSL certificate, and token signing certificate.

Trust Relationships: Establish trust relationships between AD FS and identity providers (e.g., Active Directory) and between AD FS and relying parties (applications or services).

Claim Rules: Define claim rules to transform and pass user attributes (claims) between identity providers and relying parties. Claim rules determine which information is included in the SAML tokens issued by AD FS.

Best Practices for Configuring AD FS for SSO: Following best practices can help ensure the successful configuration and deployment of AD FS for SSO:

High Availability: Deploy AD FS servers in a highly available configuration with load balancing and failover capabilities to ensure continuous availability of SSO services.

Certificate Management: Implement robust certificate management practices, including regular renewal, monitoring, and backup of SSL and token signing certificates used by AD FS.

Monitoring and Logging: Monitor AD FS server performance, SSO transactions, and security events using built-in monitoring tools, event logs, and third-party monitoring solutions.

Security Hardening: Implement security best practices, such as disabling unnecessary protocols and ciphers, enabling multi-factor authentication, and enforcing strong password policies for AD FS accounts.

Regular Testing: Conduct regular testing of SSO functionality, including authentication, authorization, and claims transformation, to identify and address any issues proactively.

Practical Examples and CLI Commands: Implementing AD FS for SSO involves various tasks and CLI commands:

Configure Federation Trust with AD FS:

phpCopy code

```
Install-ADFSFarm -CertificateThumbprint <Thumbprint> -FederationServiceName <FederationServiceName> -ServiceAccountCredential <ServiceAccountCredential> -SQLConnectionString <SQLConnectionString> -OverwriteConfiguration:$true
```

Add Relying Party Trust:

phpCopy code

```
Add-ADFSRelyingPartyTrust -Name <RelyingPartyName> -Identifier <Identifier> -WSFederation <WSFederationEndpoint>
```

Add Claim Rule:

bashCopy code

```
Add-ADFSRelyingPartyTrust -TargetName <RelyingPartyName> -ClaimRule $rule
```

Challenges and Considerations: Deploying AD FS for SSO may present challenges and considerations:

Complexity: Configuring AD FS for SSO involves multiple components, protocols, and trust relationships, which can be complex to set up and manage, especially in large and heterogeneous environments.

Integration: Integrating AD FS with existing identity and access management systems, applications, and services requires careful coordination and testing to ensure compatibility and interoperability.

Security Risks: Misconfiguration or vulnerabilities in AD FS deployments can expose organizations to security risks, such as unauthorized access, data breaches, or denial-of-service attacks.

Case Study: Configuring AD FS for SSO: Consider a scenario where an organization wants to implement SSO for its cloud-based applications using AD FS. Administrators deploy AD FS servers, configure trust relationships with Azure Active Directory, and add relying party trusts for cloud applications. They validate SSO functionality, monitor AD FS servers, and conduct regular security assessments to ensure secure and reliable SSO operations.

In summary, configuring AD FS for Single Sign-On (SSO) is a critical step in enabling seamless access to applications and services across domains and platforms. By understanding the significance of SSO, considering configuration considerations, following best practices, and leveraging CLI commands for deployment, organizations can implement robust and secure SSO solutions that enhance user experience, improve productivity, and strengthen security posture.

Active Directory Federation Services (AD FS) serves as a crucial component in modern identity and access management (IAM) solutions, facilitating seamless authentication and single sign-on (SSO) experiences across various web applications and services. This chapter explores the significance of integrating AD FS with web applications and services, considerations for deployment, best practices, and practical examples with CLI commands where applicable.

Understanding AD FS Integration with Web Applications and Services: Integrating AD FS with web applications and services enables organizations to centralize authentication, enforce access policies, and provide a seamless user experience across disparate platforms. AD FS acts as a federation service, translating authentication requests from web applications into tokens that can be validated against the organization's identity provider.

Considerations for Integration: When integrating AD FS with web applications and services, several considerations must be taken into account:

Supported Protocols: Ensure that the web applications and services support standard authentication protocols such as SAML (Security Assertion Markup Language) or WS-Federation, which are commonly used with AD FS for federated authentication.

User Experience: Consider the user experience during the authentication process, ensuring that users are seamlessly redirected to the AD FS login page and back to the web application after successful authentication.

Security Requirements: Evaluate the security requirements of the web applications and services, including encryption, token signing, and multi-factor authentication, and configure AD FS accordingly to meet those requirements.

Deployment Considerations: Deploying AD FS for integration with web applications and services involves several steps and considerations:

Certificate Management: Configure and manage SSL certificates for securing communication between AD FS servers and web applications. Certificates are essential for encrypting traffic and signing tokens exchanged during the authentication process.

Relying Party Trusts: Set up relying party trusts in AD FS for each web application or service that will be integrated. Relying party trusts define the parameters of the trust relationship between AD FS and the web application, including token issuance policies and claims transformation rules.

Claims Mapping: Define claim rules in AD FS to transform incoming claims from the identity provider (e.g., Active Directory) into the format expected by the web application. Claim rules determine which user attributes are included in the security tokens issued by AD FS.

Best Practices for Integration: Following best practices can help ensure a smooth and secure integration of AD FS with web applications and services:

Test Environment: Set up a dedicated test environment to validate the integration of AD FS with web applications before deploying changes to the production environment. Testing helps identify and address issues proactively without impacting end users.

Logging and Monitoring: Enable logging and monitoring features in AD FS to track authentication events, identify anomalies, and troubleshoot integration issues. Monitoring tools provide insights into system performance, usage patterns, and security incidents.

Scalability and Redundancy: Design the AD FS infrastructure for scalability and redundancy to handle increased authentication traffic and ensure high availability. Deploy multiple AD FS servers in a farm configuration with load balancing and failover capabilities.

User Education: Educate users about the authentication process when accessing web applications integrated with AD FS. Provide clear instructions on how to authenticate, reset passwords, and troubleshoot common authentication issues.

Practical Examples and CLI Commands: Integrating AD FS with web applications and services involves various tasks and CLI commands:

Add Relying Party Trust:

```php
phpCopy code
Add-ADFSRelyingPartyTrust -Name <RelyingPartyName> -Identifier <Identifier> -WSFederation <WSFederationEndpoint>
```

Configure Claim Rules:

```bash
bashCopy code
Add-ADFSRelyingPartyTrust -TargetName <RelyingPartyName> -ClaimRule $rule
```

View Relying Party Trusts:

```mathematica
mathematicaCopy code
Get-ADFSRelyingPartyTrust
```

Challenges and Considerations: Integrating AD FS with web applications and services may present challenges and considerations:

Compatibility Issues: Ensure that web applications and services support the authentication protocols and standards required for integration with AD FS. Incompatibility may require custom development or alternative authentication methods.

Configuration Complexity: Configuring AD FS relying party trusts, claim rules, and token issuance policies can be complex, especially for environments with multiple web applications and services. Careful planning and documentation are essential to ensure consistency and maintainability.

Security Risks: Misconfiguration of AD FS or web applications can expose organizations to security risks, such as unauthorized access, information disclosure, or denial-of-service attacks. Regular security assessments and audits are necessary to identify and remediate vulnerabilities.

Case Study: Integration of AD FS with Web Applications: Consider a scenario where an organization integrates AD FS with its cloud-based email service. Administrators configure a relying party trust in AD FS for the email service, define claim rules to map user attributes, and test the integration in a staging environment. After successful testing, the configuration is deployed to the production environment, and users can access the email service seamlessly using their corporate credentials.

In summary, integrating AD FS with web applications and services enables organizations to centralize authentication, enforce access policies, and provide a seamless user experience across diverse platforms. By considering deployment considerations, following best practices, and leveraging CLI commands for configuration tasks, organizations can implement robust and secure integration solutions that meet their business requirements and enhance user productivity.

Chapter 3: Fine-Grained Password Policies and Authentication

Fine-Grained Password Policies (FGPP) provide administrators with a granular level of control over password settings within Active Directory environments. Unlike traditional password policies that apply at the domain level, FGPP allows organizations to define multiple password policies and apply them to specific users or groups based on their security requirements. This chapter explores the significance of FGPP, considerations for implementation, best practices, and practical examples with CLI commands where applicable.

Significance of Fine-Grained Password Policies: Password policies play a crucial role in enforcing password complexity and security standards within an organization. However, traditional password policies in Active Directory are limited to a single policy per domain, which may not suffice for organizations with diverse user populations or varying security requirements. FGPP addresses this limitation by enabling administrators to define multiple password policies and apply them selectively to users or groups.

Key Components of Fine-Grained Password Policies: Fine-Grained Password Policies consist of several components that administrators can configure to define password settings tailored to specific user groups or organizational units:

Password Complexity Requirements: Define minimum password length, complexity requirements (e.g., uppercase letters, lowercase letters, numbers, special characters), and prohibited words or patterns.

Password Expiry and History: Specify password expiration settings, including maximum password age, minimum password age, and password history requirements to prevent users from reusing old passwords.

Account Lockout Policies: Configure account lockout thresholds, duration, and reset settings to protect against brute-force attacks and unauthorized access attempts.

Fine-Grained Password Policy Objects (FGPPO): Create FGPPOs using the Active Directory Administrative Center or PowerShell cmdlets to define password settings and apply them to specific users or groups.

Considerations for Implementation: Implementing Fine-Grained Password Policies requires careful planning and consideration of various factors:

User Classification: Classify users into distinct categories based on their roles, responsibilities, or security requirements. Identify user groups that require different password policies to align with their risk profiles and access privileges.

Policy Conflict Resolution: Ensure that FGPPs do not conflict with each other or with the default domain password policy. FGPPs with conflicting settings may lead to unexpected behavior or security vulnerabilities.

Testing and Validation: Test FGPPs in a controlled environment before deploying them to production. Validate password settings, account lockout policies, and password expiration behavior to ensure they meet security requirements and user expectations.

Deploying Fine-Grained Password Policies: Deploying FGPP involves several steps, including creating FGPPOs, assigning them to users or groups, and validating policy enforcement:

Create FGPPO:

sqlCopy code

```
New-ADFineGrainedPasswordPolicy -Name "PolicyName" -
ComplexityEnabled $true -MinPasswordLength 8 -
MaxPasswordAge "90.00:00:00" -PasswordHistoryCount 5
```

Assign FGPPO to Users or Groups:

sqlCopy code

```
Add-ADFineGrainedPasswordPolicySubject        -Identity
"PolicyName" -Subjects "User1", "User2"
```

Validate Policy Enforcement:
Test the applied FGPP by logging in as users assigned to the policy and verifying that password settings, such as complexity requirements, password expiration, and account lockout behavior, are enforced as expected.

Best Practices for Fine-Grained Password Policies: Following best practices can help ensure the successful implementation and management of FGPPs:

Regular Review and Updates: Periodically review FGPP settings to align with evolving security requirements, industry standards, and regulatory compliance. Update password policies as needed to address emerging threats or organizational changes.

Documentation and Auditing: Document FGPP configurations, including policy settings, assignment criteria, and justification for policy decisions. Maintain audit trails of policy changes and enforcement events for compliance and troubleshooting purposes.

Training and Awareness: Educate users about password security best practices, including creating strong passwords, safeguarding credentials, and recognizing phishing attempts. Promote awareness of FGPPs and their role in protecting sensitive information and systems.

Challenges and Considerations: Implementing and managing Fine-Grained Password Policies may present challenges and considerations:

Complexity: Managing multiple FGPPs for different user groups or organizational units can be complex and time-consuming. Ensure proper documentation, communication, and coordination among administrators to avoid policy conflicts or inconsistencies.

Policy Inheritance: Understand how FGPPs interact with other password policies, such as default domain policies or Group Policy Objects (GPOs). Incorrectly configured inheritance settings may result in unintended password policy enforcement or conflicts.

Impact on User Experience: Balance security requirements with user experience considerations to avoid overly restrictive password policies that hinder productivity or frustrate users. Solicit feedback from users and stakeholders to fine-tune password policies and address usability concerns.

Case Study: Implementing Fine-Grained Password Policies: Consider a scenario where an organization implements FGPPs to enforce stronger password security for privileged users and service accounts. Administrators create separate FGPPs with stricter complexity requirements, shorter password expiration periods, and more stringent account lockout policies for these user groups. After thorough testing and validation, the FGPPs are deployed to production, and policy enforcement is monitored regularly to ensure compliance.

In summary, Fine-Grained Password Policies provide organizations with the flexibility to tailor password settings to specific user groups or organizational units, enhancing security posture and compliance with regulatory requirements. By understanding the significance of FGPP, considering implementation considerations, following best practices, and leveraging CLI commands for deployment, organizations can implement robust password policies that balance security requirements with user experience and operational efficiency.

In today's digital landscape, ensuring robust authentication mechanisms is paramount to safeguarding sensitive information, preventing unauthorized access, and protecting against evolving cyber threats. This chapter delves into the importance of authentication mechanisms, explores various techniques for enhancing security, discusses their implementation, and provides practical examples with CLI commands where applicable.

Significance of Authentication Mechanisms: Authentication is the process of verifying the identity of users or entities attempting to access resources or services. Strong authentication mechanisms are essential for establishing trust, preventing unauthorized access, and protecting sensitive data from malicious actors. Inadequate authentication can lead to security breaches, data leaks, and compromise of critical systems.

Techniques for Enhancing Security: Enhancing security through robust authentication mechanisms involves adopting multiple layers of protection and employing advanced techniques to verify user identities and ensure secure access:

Multi-Factor Authentication (MFA): MFA requires users to provide multiple forms of identification to authenticate, such as passwords, biometrics, smart cards, or one-time passcodes (OTP). This significantly reduces the risk of unauthorized access, even if one authentication factor is compromised.

Adaptive Authentication: Adaptive authentication dynamically adjusts authentication requirements based on risk factors such as user behavior, location, device type, and time of access. This enables organizations to apply additional security measures for high-risk activities while minimizing friction for legitimate users.

Single Sign-On (SSO): SSO allows users to authenticate once and access multiple applications or services without needing to re-enter credentials. By centralizing authentication and identity management, SSO streamlines user access while enhancing security and compliance.

Biometric Authentication: Biometric authentication utilizes unique biological characteristics such as fingerprints, facial features, or iris patterns to verify user identities. Biometrics offer strong authentication while enhancing user convenience and eliminating the need for traditional passwords.

Token-Based Authentication: Token-based authentication involves issuing cryptographically secure tokens to users upon successful authentication, which are then presented for subsequent access to protected resources. Tokens can be time-bound, revocable, and encrypted to mitigate security risks.

Implementation of Authentication Mechanisms: Implementing authentication mechanisms for enhanced security requires careful planning, configuration, and integration with existing systems and applications:

MFA Configuration:

```php
phpCopy code
Enable-Mfa -User <UserName> -Method <Method1>, <Method2>
```

Adaptive Authentication Policies:

```sql
sqlCopy code
Set-AdaptiveAuthenticationPolicy -Name "PolicyName" -RiskThreshold 7 -RequireMfa $true
```

SSO Integration:

```php
phpCopy code
```

```
Configure-Sso -Application <AppName> -IdentityProvider
<IdPName>
```

Biometric Enrollment:

phpCopy code

```
Enroll-Biometric -User <UserName> -Type <BiometricType>
```

Token Generation and Verification:

sqlCopy code

```
Generate-Token -User <UserName> -Validity 3600 -
Scope <Scope>
```

Best Practices for Implementation: Implementing authentication mechanisms effectively requires adherence to best practices and security guidelines:

Risk-Based Approach: Assess the risk profile of users, applications, and transactions to determine appropriate authentication mechanisms and security controls. Implement adaptive authentication policies to dynamically adjust security requirements based on risk factors.

User Education: Educate users about the importance of strong authentication practices, such as choosing complex passwords, safeguarding credentials, and recognizing phishing attempts. Provide clear instructions on how to enroll in MFA, biometric authentication, or other security features.

Continuous Monitoring: Monitor authentication logs, audit trails, and security events to detect anomalies, suspicious activities, or unauthorized access attempts. Implement real-time alerts and automated response mechanisms to mitigate security incidents promptly.

Compliance and Standards: Ensure compliance with industry regulations and security standards such as GDPR, HIPAA, PCI DSS, and NIST guidelines. Implement authentication mechanisms that align with regulatory requirements and industry best practices to protect sensitive data and maintain trust.

Regular Updates and Patch Management: Keep authentication systems, protocols, and libraries up-to-date with the latest security patches and updates. Address known vulnerabilities promptly to mitigate the risk of exploitation by malicious actors.

Challenges and Considerations: Implementing authentication mechanisms for enhanced security may present challenges and considerations:

User Experience vs. Security: Balancing security requirements with user experience is critical to ensure acceptance and adoption of authentication mechanisms. Striking the right balance between security and usability can be challenging, especially for organizations with diverse user populations.

Integration Complexity: Integrating authentication mechanisms with existing systems, applications, and infrastructure may require extensive customization, configuration, and testing. Ensure compatibility, interoperability, and seamless user experience across different platforms and devices.

Regulatory Compliance: Compliance with regulatory requirements such as GDPR, PCI DSS, and HIPAA adds complexity to authentication implementations. Ensure that authentication mechanisms meet regulatory standards for data protection, privacy, and access control.

Emerging Threats: Stay vigilant against emerging cyber threats, including phishing attacks, credential stuffing, and account takeover attempts. Implement proactive security measures such as threat intelligence, anomaly detection, and user behavior analytics to mitigate risks effectively.

Case Study: Implementing MFA for Enhanced Security: Consider a scenario where an organization implements MFA to enhance security for remote access to corporate resources. Administrators configure MFA policies to require users to authenticate using both passwords and one-time passcodes generated by mobile authenticator apps. The implementation significantly reduces the risk of unauthorized access and strengthens the organization's security posture.

In summary, implementing authentication mechanisms for enhanced security is essential for protecting against evolving cyber threats, safeguarding sensitive information, and ensuring compliance with regulatory requirements. By adopting multiple layers of protection, leveraging advanced techniques such as MFA, adaptive authentication, and biometrics, and following best practices for implementation, organizations can establish a robust security framework that balances security, usability, and compliance requirements effectively.

Chapter 4: Advanced Group Policy Management

Group Policy Preferences (GPP) and Item-Level Targeting (ILT) are powerful features of Microsoft's Group Policy infrastructure that allow administrators to configure and manage settings on Windows-based systems with precision and flexibility. Next, we explore the significance of GPP and ILT, their deployment, and practical examples with CLI commands where applicable.

Understanding Group Policy Preferences (GPP): Group Policy Preferences extend the capabilities of traditional Group Policy Objects (GPOs) by providing administrators with a more granular approach to configure settings on target computers. Unlike policy settings enforced by GPOs, GPPs allow administrators to set preferences that users can change, providing greater flexibility while maintaining central management control.

Key Features of Group Policy Preferences: GPP offers several key features that differentiate it from traditional GPO settings:

User Preferences: Administrators can configure preferences for users, such as mapped network drives, printers, registry settings, and shortcuts, which users can modify without violating Group Policy settings.

Computer Preferences: GPP enables administrators to configure settings on target computers, including network shares, scheduled tasks, local users and groups, and environment variables, providing greater flexibility in managing system configurations.

Item-Level Targeting: ILT allows administrators to apply preferences selectively based on specified conditions, such as user attributes, group membership, computer properties,

IP address ranges, or time of day, enabling highly targeted configuration management.

Deploying Group Policy Preferences: Deploying GPP involves several steps, including creating preference items, configuring settings, and applying them to target computers or users:

Create Preference Item:

sqlCopy code

New-GPO -Name "PreferenceItemName" -ItemType <ItemType>

Configure Preference Settings:

mathematicaCopy code

Set-GPRegistryValue -Name "PreferenceItemName" -KeyPath <RegistryKeyPath> -ValueName <ValueName> -Value <Value> -Type <ValueType>

Apply Preference Item:

mathematicaCopy code

Add-GPRegistryValue -Name "PreferenceItemName" -TargetName <TargetComputer> -Path <RegistryPath>

Item-Level Targeting:

mathematicaCopy code

Set-GPItemLevelTargeting -Item "PreferenceItemName" -Target <TargetCriteria>

Understanding Item-Level Targeting (ILT): Item-Level Targeting enhances the precision of GPP by allowing administrators to apply preferences based on specific conditions or criteria. ILT evaluates targeting conditions at runtime and applies preference settings only if the specified criteria are met, providing greater flexibility and control over configuration management.

Key Features of Item-Level Targeting: ILT offers several key features that enable administrators to target preference settings with precision:

User and Computer Targeting: ILT supports targeting based on user attributes (e.g., group membership, organizational unit) and computer properties (e.g., operating system version, hardware configuration), enabling tailored configuration management for different user groups and computer types.

Time-Based Targeting: Administrators can configure preferences to apply at specific times or intervals, allowing for scheduled configuration changes or maintenance tasks.

Location-Based Targeting: ILT supports targeting based on IP address ranges or network locations, enabling administrators to apply preferences selectively to users or computers in specific geographic locations or network segments.

Security Group Targeting: ILT enables targeting based on membership in security groups, allowing administrators to apply preferences to users or computers with specific security permissions or roles.

Practical Examples and CLI Commands: Implementing GPP and ILT involves configuring preference items and targeting criteria using CLI commands:

Create Registry Preference Item:

phpCopy code

```
New-GPRegistryValue -Action Create -Key <RegistryKey> -ValueName <ValueName> -Value <Value> -Type <ValueType> -Context <UserOrComputer>
```

Apply Preference Item with ILT:

mathematicaCopy code

```
Set-GPItemLevelTargeting -Item "PreferenceItemName" -Target "UserInSecurityGroup" -Path "\\DomainController\SecurityGroup"
```

Best Practices for Deployment: Deploying GPP and ILT effectively requires adherence to best practices and considerations:

Test Environment: Test preference settings and targeting criteria in a controlled environment before deploying them to production. Validate configuration changes to ensure they behave as expected and do not disrupt user productivity.

Documentation and Version Control: Document GPP and ILT configurations, including preference items, targeting criteria, and rationale for configuration decisions. Maintain version control of GPOs and preference items to track changes and facilitate troubleshooting.

Security Considerations: Ensure that preference settings and targeting criteria adhere to security best practices and do not expose sensitive information or compromise system integrity. Limit access to GPP and ILT configurations to authorized administrators to prevent unauthorized changes.

Monitoring and Auditing: Monitor GPP and ILT configurations, audit changes, and review event logs regularly to detect anomalies, unauthorized modifications, or misconfigurations. Implement alerting mechanisms to notify administrators of critical events or security incidents.

Challenges and Considerations: Implementing GPP and ILT may present challenges and considerations:

Complexity: Managing a large number of preference items and targeting criteria can be complex and challenging to maintain. Adopt a systematic approach to organization, documentation, and version control to streamline management and troubleshooting.

Performance Impact: Applying preference settings and targeting criteria at runtime may introduce performance overhead, especially in large environments with numerous GPOs and preference items. Monitor system performance and optimize configuration settings to minimize impact on user experience and system resources.

Compatibility Issues: Ensure compatibility of preference settings and targeting criteria with target operating systems, applications, and infrastructure components. Test configurations across diverse environments to identify compatibility issues and address them proactively.

User Experience: Balance configuration management requirements with user experience considerations to avoid disrupting productivity or causing user frustration. Communicate changes effectively, provide user training and support, and solicit feedback to optimize preference settings and targeting criteria.

Case Study: Implementing Group Policy Preferences with ILT: Consider a scenario where an organization deploys GPP with ILT to configure network drive mappings for different user groups. Administrators create preference items for each user group and apply ILT based on group membership. Users automatically receive mapped network drives based on their group affiliation, streamlining access to shared resources while ensuring data security and compliance.

In summary, Group Policy Preferences and Item-Level Targeting offer powerful capabilities for configuring and managing settings on Windows-based systems with precision and flexibility. By understanding their significance, deploying them effectively, and following best practices for configuration management, organizations can streamline administrative tasks, enhance configuration consistency, and improve overall system security and compliance.

Group Policy (GP) is a powerful tool used in Windows environments to enforce settings, configurations, and security policies across multiple computers and users. However, despite its robustness, administrators often encounter challenges related to GP application, leading to issues such as settings not being applied, inconsistent behavior across systems, or unexpected results. Next, we delve into troubleshooting techniques for addressing common GP application issues, exploring various strategies,

CLI commands, and practical examples to diagnose and resolve problems effectively.

Understanding Group Policy Application: Before delving into troubleshooting techniques, it's essential to understand how Group Policy is applied in Windows environments. Group Policy settings are typically processed in the following order: Local Group Policy, Site-linked Group Policy, Domain-linked Group Policy, and Organizational Unit (OU)-linked Group Policy. Settings are inherited from parent containers (e.g., domain, OU) and applied in the order of LSDOU (Local, Site, Domain, OU).

Common Group Policy Application Issues: Group Policy application issues can manifest in various ways, including:

Settings Not Applied: GP settings fail to apply to target computers or users, leading to inconsistent configurations or security vulnerabilities.

Slow Processing: Group Policy processing takes an unusually long time, causing delays in system startup or user logon.

Inheritance Problems: Settings from parent containers (e.g., domain-level policies) override settings from child containers (e.g., OU-level policies), leading to unexpected behavior.

Loopback Processing Issues: Loopback processing, which applies user settings based on computer configuration or vice versa, may result in conflicts or unintended consequences.

Permission Problems: Incorrect permissions on Group Policy objects (GPOs) or related Active Directory objects may prevent policy application or lead to access denied errors.

Troubleshooting Techniques: To effectively troubleshoot Group Policy application issues, administrators can employ a systematic approach, including:

Review Event Logs: Start by examining event logs on target computers and domain controllers for errors, warnings, or informational messages related to Group Policy processing.

Event Viewer (eventvwr) is a useful tool for accessing event logs.

Group Policy Modeling and Results: Use the Group Policy Management Console (GPMC) to run Group Policy Modeling and Group Policy Results Wizard to simulate and analyze Group Policy application for specific users or computers. This helps identify discrepancies between expected and actual policy settings.

Diagnostic Logging: Enable diagnostic logging for Group Policy processing using the Group Policy Operational log (gplogview) to capture detailed information about policy processing steps, including applied settings, filtering, and policy precedence.

Resultant Set of Policy (RSoP): Use the Resultant Set of Policy (RSoP) tool (rsop.msc) to generate reports showing applied Group Policy settings for a specific user or computer. RSoP provides insight into which policies are being applied and from which GPOs.

GPUpdate and GPResult: Run the gpupdate /force command on target computers to force immediate Group Policy refresh. Then, use the gpresult /r command to view the resultant set of applied Group Policy settings and verify whether the expected settings are being applied.

CLI Commands and Practical Examples: Troubleshooting Group Policy application issues often involves using CLI commands to gather information, diagnose problems, and implement solutions. Here are some examples:

Check Group Policy Status:
bashCopy code

```
gpresult /r
```

Force Group Policy Update:
bashCopy code

```
gpupdate /force
```

Enable Diagnostic Logging:
bashCopy code

```
auditpol    /set    /subcategory:"Detailed    Tracking"
/success:enable /failure:enable
```

View Group Policy Operational Log:
mathematicaCopy code

```
Get-WinEvent    -LogName    "Microsoft-Windows-
GroupPolicy/Operational"
```

Best Practices for Troubleshooting: When troubleshooting Group Policy application issues, it's essential to follow best practices to ensure efficient and effective resolution:

Document Configuration Changes: Maintain detailed documentation of Group Policy settings, configurations, and changes to track modifications and facilitate troubleshooting.

Test in Isolated Environment: Use a test environment to replicate and troubleshoot Group Policy issues without impacting production systems. This allows administrators to experiment with different solutions and validate their effectiveness.

Engage Support Resources: Leverage online resources, forums, and vendor support channels for assistance with complex Group Policy problems. Collaborate with colleagues and peers to share insights and solutions to common challenges.

Implement Change Control: Adhere to change management processes when making modifications to Group Policy settings or configurations. Document change requests, obtain approvals, and communicate changes to stakeholders to mitigate the risk of unintended consequences.

Monitor and Review Regularly: Establish proactive monitoring practices to detect and address Group Policy issues before they escalate. Conduct periodic reviews of

Group Policy settings, configurations, and performance to identify opportunities for optimization and improvement.

Troubleshooting Group Policy application issues requires a combination of technical expertise, diagnostic tools, and systematic approaches. By understanding common issues, employing effective troubleshooting techniques, leveraging CLI commands, and following best practices, administrators can diagnose and resolve Group Policy problems efficiently, ensuring the consistent application of settings and configurations across Windows environments.

Chapter 5: Active Directory Domain Services (AD DS) Deployment and Optimization

Deploying Active Directory Domain Controllers (DCs) is a critical aspect of building and maintaining a robust Windows network infrastructure. DCs play a central role in authentication, authorization, and directory services, serving as the backbone of the Active Directory (AD) environment. Next, we explore the planning process, deployment considerations, and practical techniques for executing successful Active Directory Domain Controller deployments, including CLI commands where applicable.

Understanding Active Directory Domain Controllers: Active Directory Domain Controllers are servers running the Windows Server operating system with the Active Directory Domain Services (AD DS) role installed. They store directory data, authenticate users, enforce security policies, and facilitate replication of directory information across the network.

Planning for Domain Controller Deployments: Planning is a critical phase of any domain controller deployment project. It involves assessing organizational requirements, designing the AD topology, and determining the placement and configuration of domain controllers. Key considerations include:

Topology Design: Determine the forest and domain structure, including the number of domains, domain controllers per domain, and placement of domain controllers across physical locations to ensure fault tolerance and scalability.

Hardware Requirements: Evaluate hardware specifications, including CPU, RAM, storage, and network bandwidth, based on anticipated workloads, user counts, and replication requirements.

Site and Replication Design: Define Active Directory sites and site links to optimize replication traffic and ensure efficient communication between domain controllers in geographically distributed environments.

High Availability and Disaster Recovery: Implement redundancy and fault tolerance mechanisms, such as deploying multiple domain controllers per domain, configuring backup domain controllers, and establishing disaster recovery procedures.

Deployment Techniques and CLI Commands: Deploying Active Directory Domain Controllers involves several steps, including installing the AD DS role, promoting the server to a domain controller, and configuring AD DS settings. Here are some CLI commands and techniques for executing domain controller deployments:

Install AD DS Role:

mathematicaCopy code

```
Install-WindowsFeature -Name AD-Domain-Services -IncludeManagementTools
```

Promote Server to Domain Controller:

mathematicaCopy code

```
Install-ADDSDomainController -DomainName <DomainName> -Credential (Get-Credential) -InstallDns -NoGlobalCatalog -SiteName <SiteName>
```

Configure DNS Settings:

mathematicaCopy code

```
Set-DnsServerForwarder -IPAddress <ForwarderIPAddress>
```

Configure Sites and Subnets:

phpCopy code

```
New-ADReplicationSite -Name <SiteName>
```

Best Practices for Deployment: Deploying Active Directory Domain Controllers requires adherence to best practices to ensure stability, security, and optimal performance:

Standardization: Follow standardized deployment procedures and configurations to maintain consistency across domain controllers and minimize compatibility issues.

Security Hardening: Implement security best practices, such as regular patching, least privilege access controls, and disabling unnecessary services, to mitigate security risks and vulnerabilities.

Monitoring and Maintenance: Implement monitoring solutions to track the health and performance of domain controllers, including monitoring event logs, replication status, and resource utilization. Perform regular maintenance tasks, such as database defragmentation and backup, to ensure the integrity of AD DS.

Capacity Planning: Anticipate future growth and scalability requirements when deploying domain controllers, ensuring that hardware resources and AD DS configurations can accommodate increasing workloads and user counts.

Documentation and Training: Maintain comprehensive documentation of domain controller configurations, deployment procedures, and troubleshooting steps. Provide training to IT staff responsible for managing and maintaining Active Directory to ensure proficiency in domain controller administration.

Challenges and Considerations: Deploying Active Directory Domain Controllers may encounter challenges and considerations that require careful planning and mitigation:

Network Connectivity: Ensure reliable network connectivity between domain controllers, especially in distributed environments with multiple sites and network segments. Implement redundant network paths and optimize bandwidth utilization for replication traffic.

Legacy System Integration: Address compatibility issues and dependencies with legacy systems or applications that rely on specific Active Directory configurations or functionalities. Plan migration strategies and compatibility testing to minimize disruption to existing services.

Security Compliance: Align domain controller deployments with organizational security policies, compliance regulations, and industry standards. Implement encryption, access controls, and auditing mechanisms to protect sensitive data and ensure regulatory compliance.

Resource Constraints: Allocate adequate resources, including CPU, memory, and storage, to domain controllers based on workload requirements and expected user activity. Monitor resource utilization and performance metrics to identify and address resource constraints proactively.

Planning and executing Active Directory Domain Controller deployments are critical tasks that require careful consideration, meticulous planning, and adherence to best practices. By following standardized deployment procedures, leveraging CLI commands and techniques, and addressing key considerations such as topology design, high availability, and security compliance, organizations can deploy domain controllers effectively, ensuring a stable and resilient Active Directory environment.

Active Directory Domain Services (AD DS) replication and site topology play a crucial role in ensuring the reliability, performance, and scalability of a Windows network environment. Efficient replication and well-designed site topology are essential for maintaining data consistency, minimizing latency, and optimizing resource utilization across distributed Active Directory deployments. Next, we explore techniques, best practices, and CLI commands for optimizing AD DS replication and site topology to achieve optimal performance and reliability.

Understanding AD DS Replication: AD DS replication is the process of synchronizing directory data between domain controllers within the same domain or across different domains in a forest. Replication ensures that changes made to directory objects, such as user accounts, group memberships, and Group Policy settings, are propagated efficiently and consistently throughout the Active Directory infrastructure.

Factors Affecting Replication Performance: Several factors can impact the performance and efficiency of AD DS replication:

Topology Design: The topology of Active Directory sites and site links influences replication traffic patterns and determines how domain controllers communicate with each other.

Network Infrastructure: Network bandwidth, latency, and reliability affect the speed and reliability of replication traffic between domain controllers, especially in distributed environments with geographically dispersed sites.

Replication Schedule: Replication intervals and schedules configured for site links and connections determine how frequently changes are replicated between domain controllers and impact the freshness of directory data.

Directory Object Changes: The frequency and volume of changes made to directory objects by administrators or users affect the workload and replication traffic generated by domain controllers.

Optimizing AD DS Replication: Optimizing AD DS replication involves implementing strategies to minimize latency, reduce replication traffic, and ensure data consistency across domain controllers:

Site Topology Optimization: Design an efficient Active Directory site topology that reflects the organization's network infrastructure, geographic locations, and replication requirements. Create sites, site links, and site link bridges to optimize replication traffic flow and minimize latency.

Replication Schedule Adjustment: Adjust replication schedules and intervals based on network bandwidth availability, usage patterns, and directory object change rates. Configure frequent replication for critical data and less frequent replication for less critical data to balance workload and resource utilization.

Replication Monitoring and Troubleshooting: Monitor replication status, latency, and errors using tools such as Repadmin and Active Directory Replication Status Tool (ADREPLSTATUS). Identify and troubleshoot replication issues promptly to prevent data inconsistency and ensure replication health.

Bandwidth Management: Implement bandwidth management solutions, such as Quality of Service (QoS) policies or network throttling, to prioritize replication traffic and prevent it from consuming excessive network resources, especially in bandwidth-constrained environments.

Active Directory Sites and Services Optimization: Use Active Directory Sites and Services (Dssite.msc) to manage site topology, site links, and replication connections. Ensure that domain controllers are correctly assigned to sites and that replication connections are configured optimally based on network proximity and connectivity.

Replication Compression and Encryption: Enable replication compression and encryption to reduce replication traffic overhead and enhance data security during transit. Configure replication settings to use compression and encryption algorithms supported by domain controllers and network infrastructure.

CLI Commands and Techniques: CLI commands are instrumental in optimizing AD DS replication and site topology. Here are some examples:

View Replication Status:

```
bashCopy code
repadmin /showrepl
```

Force Replication:

```
bashCopy code
repadmin /syncall /AdeP
```

Check Replication Latency:

```
bashCopy code
repadmin /replsum
```

Monitor Replication Traffic:

```
bashCopy code
repadmin /istg
```

Configure Site Links:

```
bashCopy code
nltest /dclist:<DomainName>
```

Troubleshoot Replication Issues:

```
bashCopy code
repadmin /showrepl <DestinationDC>
```

Best Practices for Optimization: Adhering to best practices is essential for optimizing AD DS replication and site topology effectively:

Regular Monitoring and Maintenance: Monitor replication status, latency, and errors regularly using automated tools and scripts. Perform routine maintenance tasks, such as database defragmentation and server health checks, to keep domain controllers in optimal condition.

Capacity Planning: Anticipate future growth and scalability requirements when designing site topology and configuring replication settings. Ensure that the infrastructure can accommodate increasing workloads and directory object changes without compromising performance or data consistency.

Documentation and Knowledge Sharing: Document site topology designs, replication configurations, and optimization strategies. Share knowledge and best practices with IT staff and stakeholders to foster collaboration and ensure consistency in replication management.

Testing and Validation: Test site topology changes, replication configuration updates, and optimization techniques in a controlled environment before deploying them to production. Validate changes using pilot deployments or staging environments to identify potential issues and mitigate risks.

Continuous Improvement: Continuously evaluate and refine replication optimization strategies based on feedback, performance metrics, and changes in organizational requirements. Implement iterative improvements to site topology, replication schedules, and network infrastructure to adapt to evolving business needs and technology advancements.

Optimizing AD DS replication and site topology is essential for maintaining a reliable, efficient, and scalable Active Directory infrastructure. By implementing best practices, leveraging CLI commands and techniques, and monitoring replication performance regularly, organizations can ensure data consistency, minimize latency, and maximize the performance of domain controllers across distributed environments.

Chapter 6: Active Directory Lightweight Directory Services (AD LDS)

Active Directory Lightweight Directory Services (AD LDS), formerly known as Active Directory Application Mode (ADAM), provides directory services that are separate from the Active Directory Domain Services (AD DS) used in traditional Windows environments. AD LDS instances are lightweight, flexible, and designed for scenarios where a full AD DS deployment is not required. Next, we explore the process of deploying and configuring AD LDS instances, including CLI commands and deployment techniques, to set up directory services tailored to specific application requirements.

Understanding AD LDS: AD LDS is a directory service that provides lightweight directory access protocol (LDAP) functionality, similar to AD DS, but without the overhead of a full domain infrastructure. It allows organizations to deploy directory services for applications, services, or data stores that require LDAP authentication and directory capabilities without the need for a domain controller.

Deployment Planning: Before deploying AD LDS instances, it's essential to assess the requirements of the applications or services that will utilize the directory service. Considerations include:

Application Integration: Determine how the AD LDS instance will be integrated with existing applications or services. Identify LDAP requirements, schema extensions, and authentication mechanisms needed to support application functionality.

Data Partitioning: Plan the structure of the AD LDS instance's directory partitions (also known as naming contexts) based on data segregation requirements. Define separate partitions for different application data sets or organizational units to ensure data isolation and access control.

High Availability: Consider deployment strategies for ensuring high availability and fault tolerance of the AD LDS instance. Implement redundancy, load balancing, or failover mechanisms to minimize service disruption and downtime.

Deploying AD LDS Instances: Deploying AD LDS instances involves several steps, including installing the AD LDS role, creating an instance, configuring instance settings, and initializing the directory partition. Here are some CLI commands and techniques for deploying AD LDS instances:

Install AD LDS Role:

mathematicaCopy code

```
Install-WindowsFeature -Name ADLDS
```

Create AD LDS Instance:

bashCopy code

```
dsmgmt.exe /N /addinstance /instancename:<InstanceName> /instpwd:<Password> /ldapport:<LDAPPort> /sslport:<SSLPort>
```

Configure AD LDS Instance Settings:

Copy code

```
dsdbutil.exe
```

(Enter into the DSDBUTIL command prompt)

Copy code

```
metadata cleanup
```

(Execute metadata cleanup commands to configure instance settings)

Initialize Directory Partition:

cssCopy code

```
ldifde.exe -i -f <LDIFFileName>
```

(Import LDIF files to initialize directory partitions)

Configuring AD LDS Instances: Once the AD LDS instance is deployed, configure settings and parameters based on application requirements and organizational policies. Configuration tasks may include:

Schema Customization: Extend the AD LDS schema to support custom attributes, object classes, or LDAP filters required by applications. Use tools such as LDIF files, ADSI Edit, or LDIFDE to modify the schema.

Authentication and Authorization: Configure authentication mechanisms, access control lists (ACLs), and permissions to control user access to directory data. Implement authentication protocols such as LDAP simple bind, LDAP over SSL (LDAPS), or Windows Integrated Authentication based on security requirements.

Replication and Synchronization: Set up replication agreements between AD LDS instances or synchronize data with external directory services using LDAP synchronization protocols such as LDAP Data Interchange Format (LDIF) or Lightweight Directory Access Protocol (LDAP) replication.

Security Hardening: Implement security best practices to protect the AD LDS instance from unauthorized access, data breaches, or denial-of-service attacks. Secure communication channels using SSL/TLS encryption, enable audit logging, and restrict access to sensitive directory data.

CLI Commands and Techniques: CLI commands are instrumental in deploying and configuring AD LDS instances. Here are some examples:

Create AD LDS Instance:

bashCopy code

dsmgmt.exe /N /addinstance /instancename:MyInstance /instpwd:Password123 /ldapport:50000 /sslport:50001

Start AD LDS Service:

sqlCopy code

net start MSADDS

Configure Schema Extension:

cssCopy code

ldifde -i -f SchemaExtension .ldf

Set ACLs for Directory Objects:

arduinoCopy code

dsacls   "cn=MyObject,ou=MyOU,dc=MyInstance,dc=com" /G "Domain Admins:GA"

Best Practices for Configuration: When configuring AD LDS instances, adhere to best practices to ensure security, performance, and reliability:

Regular Backup and Maintenance: Implement backup procedures to protect directory data and configuration settings. Perform regular maintenance tasks, such as database defragmentation and schema cleanup, to optimize performance and prevent data corruption.

Documentation and Change Management: Document configuration settings, schema modifications, and deployment procedures. Maintain a change management process to track changes, approvals, and rollbacks to ensure consistency and accountability.

Performance Monitoring: Monitor AD LDS instance performance metrics, such as CPU utilization, memory usage, and LDAP query response times. Use performance monitoring tools, event logs, and diagnostic utilities to identify bottlenecks and optimize resource allocation.

Integration Testing: Test AD LDS integration with applications, services, or data stores in a controlled environment before deploying to production. Validate functionality, data consistency, and performance under different load conditions to ensure reliability and compatibility.

Deploying and configuring AD LDS instances requires careful planning, deployment, and configuration to meet the needs of applications, services, and organizational requirements. By following best practices, leveraging CLI commands and techniques, and adhering to security and performance guidelines, organizations can deploy AD LDS instances effectively, providing scalable, reliable, and secure directory services for their applications and users.

Active Directory Lightweight Directory Services (AD LDS) provides a flexible and lightweight directory solution that can be seamlessly integrated with various applications and services to support authentication, authorization, and directory lookup functionalities. Next, we explore the process of integrating AD LDS with applications and services, including CLI commands and deployment techniques, to leverage its directory capabilities effectively.

Understanding AD LDS Integration: AD LDS integration involves configuring applications and services to interact with the AD LDS directory service for user authentication, attribute lookup, and access control. By integrating with AD LDS, applications can leverage a centralized directory infrastructure without the need for a full Active Directory Domain Services (AD DS) deployment.

Integration Planning: Before integrating AD LDS with applications and services, it's essential to conduct thorough planning to understand integration requirements, including:

Authentication Mechanisms: Determine the authentication protocols and mechanisms supported by the application or service, such as LDAP bind, LDAP simple bind, LDAP over SSL (LDAPS), or Windows Integrated Authentication.

Attribute Mapping: Identify the directory attributes required by the application for user authentication, authorization, and profile management. Map application attributes to corresponding AD LDS attributes to ensure data consistency and compatibility.

Access Control Requirements: Define access control policies and permissions for application users based on role-based access control (RBAC) or organizational requirements. Configure ACLs and security groups in AD LDS to enforce access controls and restrict unauthorized access.

Integrating AD LDS with Applications: Integrating AD LDS with applications involves configuring application settings, authentication mechanisms, and directory connections to enable seamless interaction with the directory service. Here are some CLI commands and techniques for integrating AD LDS with applications:

Configure Application Settings: Use application-specific configuration files or settings to specify the LDAP server address, port number, bind credentials, and search base DN for connecting to the AD LDS instance.

Authenticate Users: Implement authentication logic in the application code to authenticate users against the AD LDS directory using LDAP bind operations or other supported authentication mechanisms.

Query Directory Data: Use LDAP search queries or directory lookup APIs to retrieve user attributes, group memberships, or organizational information from the AD LDS directory for user authentication, authorization, or profile management.

Implement Single Sign-On (SSO): Enable SSO capabilities by integrating AD LDS with identity federation services, such as Active Directory Federation Services (AD FS) or third-party identity providers. Configure trust relationships and authentication protocols to enable seamless authentication across multiple applications.

CLI Commands and Techniques: CLI commands play a crucial role in configuring AD LDS integration with applications and services. Here are some examples:

Create Application Service Account:

sqlCopy code

```
dsadd user "cn=AppService,ou=ServiceAccounts,dc=example,dc=com" -samid AppService -upn AppService@example.com -pwd P@ssw0rd
```

Grant Application Access Rights:

csharpCopy code

```
dsadd group "cn=AppUsers,ou=Groups,dc=example,dc=com" dsmod group "cn=AppUsers,ou=Groups,dc=example,dc=com" -addmbr "cn=AppService,ou=ServiceAccounts,dc=example,dc=com"
```

Configure LDAP Connection Settings:

phpCopy code

```
ldapsearch -H ldap://<ADLDS_Server>:<Port> -D <BindDN> -w <Password> -b <BaseDN> -s sub "(objectclass=*)"
```

Query Directory Data:

phpCopy code

```
ldapsearch -H ldap://<ADLDS_Server>:<Port> -D <BindDN> -w <Password> -b "ou=Users,dc=example,dc=com" -s sub "(cn=User1)"
```

Best Practices for Integration: When integrating AD LDS with applications and services, consider the following best practices:

Secure Communication: Enable SSL/TLS encryption to secure communication between the application and the AD LDS directory. Use LDAPS or StartTLS protocols to encrypt LDAP traffic and prevent unauthorized access or data interception.

Granular Access Controls: Implement fine-grained access controls and permissions in AD LDS to restrict access to sensitive directory data. Define security groups, role-based access policies, and attribute-level permissions based on the principle of least privilege.

Error Handling and Logging: Implement robust error handling and logging mechanisms in the application code to capture authentication failures, directory lookup errors, and connection issues. Log events and exceptions for troubleshooting and auditing purposes.

Scalability and Performance: Design the application architecture to scale efficiently and handle increased user loads. Implement connection pooling, caching mechanisms, and load balancing strategies to distribute authentication requests and optimize performance.

Regular Testing and Validation: Test integration scenarios in a controlled environment to validate functionality, performance, and security. Conduct integration testing, user acceptance testing (UAT), and security assessments to identify and address potential issues before deploying to production.

Integrating AD LDS with applications and services enables organizations to leverage the directory capabilities of AD LDS for user authentication, authorization, and directory lookup functionalities. By following best practices, leveraging CLI commands and techniques, and ensuring secure and reliable integration, organizations can enhance the functionality, scalability, and security of their applications while leveraging the flexibility and lightweight nature of AD LDS.

Chapter 7: Active Directory Certificate Services (AD CS) Implementation

Active Directory Certificate Services (AD CS) is a Windows Server role that enables organizations to establish a public key infrastructure (PKI) and issue digital certificates for secure communication, authentication, and data encryption. Planning and deploying AD CS involves careful consideration of PKI requirements, certificate issuance policies, infrastructure design, and deployment best practices. Next, we delve into the process of planning and deploying AD CS, including CLI commands and deployment techniques, to establish a robust PKI infrastructure tailored to organizational needs.

Understanding AD CS: AD CS provides a set of services for creating, managing, and distributing digital certificates within an organization. These certificates are used to verify the identity of users, computers, and devices, encrypt data, and establish secure communication channels over networks. AD CS includes components such as Certification Authorities (CAs), certificate templates, enrollment services, and certificate revocation mechanisms.

Planning for AD CS Deployment: Before deploying AD CS, organizations must assess their PKI requirements and define the scope of the deployment. Key considerations include:

Certificate Types: Determine the types of certificates required for various use cases, such as user authentication, device authentication, secure email, code signing, and server authentication. Define certificate templates and issuance policies based on organizational needs and compliance requirements.

Infrastructure Design: Design the AD CS infrastructure to ensure scalability, fault tolerance, and performance. Decide whether to deploy a single-tier or multi-tier CA hierarchy, select hardware and software requirements, and plan for redundancy, load balancing, and disaster recovery.

Security and Compliance: Address security considerations such as key management, certificate lifecycle management, access control, and compliance with regulatory standards (e.g., GDPR, HIPAA, PCI DSS). Implement measures to protect private keys, secure certificate enrollment, and enforce certificate usage policies.

Deploying AD CS: Deploying AD CS involves several steps, including installing the AD CS role, configuring CAs, enrolling certificates, and establishing trust relationships with clients. Here are some CLI commands and techniques for deploying AD CS:

Install AD CS Role:

mathematicaCopy code

```
Install-WindowsFeature -Name ADCS-Cert-Authority -IncludeManagementTools
```

Configure CA Role:

sqlCopy code

```
Add-WindowsFeature ADCS-Cert-Authority
```

Install Certificate Authority:

mathematicaCopy code

```
Install-AdcsCertificationAuthority -CAType EnterpriseRootCA
```

Configure Certificate Templates:

Copy code

```
certtmpl.msc
```

Enroll Certificates:

arduinoCopy code

```
certreq -submit -attrib "CertificateTemplateName:WebServer" -attrib
```

"Subject:CN=www.example.com"   -attrib
"SAN:DNS=www.example.com&DNS=example.com"

Configuration and Management: After deploying AD CS, configure certificate templates, enrollment policies, and certificate revocation mechanisms to meet organizational requirements:

Certificate Templates: Customize certificate templates to define key usage, validity periods, subject names, and other attributes. Specify enrollment restrictions, autoenrollment settings, and certificate renewal policies based on application and security requirements.

Certificate Enrollment: Configure certificate enrollment services, such as Certificate Enrollment Web Services (CEWS) or Certificate Enrollment Policy Web Service (CEP), to automate certificate issuance and renewal for users and devices. Enable autoenrollment policies to streamline the enrollment process and ensure certificate compliance.

Certificate Revocation: Implement certificate revocation mechanisms, such as Certificate Revocation Lists (CRLs) or Online Certificate Status Protocol (OCSP), to revoke compromised or expired certificates. Configure CRL publication points, distribution points, and OCSP responders to provide timely revocation information to clients.

Key Management: Securely manage private keys, certificate stores, and cryptographic operations to prevent unauthorized access and ensure the integrity of certificate operations. Implement hardware security modules (HSMs), key archival, and key recovery mechanisms to protect sensitive cryptographic assets.

Monitoring and Maintenance: Regular monitoring and maintenance are essential for ensuring the reliability, availability, and security of the AD CS infrastructure:

Event Logging: Monitor AD CS events, audit logs, and performance counters to detect security incidents, certificate enrollment failures, or performance issues. Use tools such as Event Viewer, PowerShell scripts, or third-party monitoring solutions to track AD CS activities.

Certificate Lifecycle Management: Implement processes for certificate lifecycle management, including certificate issuance, renewal, revocation, and expiration. Monitor certificate expiration dates, renew certificates before they expire, and revoke certificates promptly when compromised or no longer needed.

Backup and Recovery: Implement backup and recovery procedures for AD CS components, including CA databases, private keys, configuration settings, and certificate templates. Regularly backup CA databases and archive private keys to protect against data loss or corruption.

Patch Management: Keep AD CS servers up to date with the latest security patches, hotfixes, and updates from Microsoft. Implement patch management policies to regularly apply patches, perform vulnerability assessments, and mitigate potential security risks.

Planning and deploying Active Directory Certificate Services (AD CS) is critical for establishing a robust PKI infrastructure that supports secure communication, authentication, and data encryption within an organization. By following best practices, leveraging CLI commands and deployment techniques, and implementing robust configuration and management processes, organizations can deploy AD CS effectively and ensure the integrity, confidentiality, and availability of their digital certificates and cryptographic assets.

Certificate authorities (CAs) play a crucial role in establishing trust within a public key infrastructure (PKI) by issuing and managing digital certificates. Managing certificate authority hierarchies and key lifecycle involves defining the CA hierarchy, configuring trust relationships, securing private keys, and implementing key lifecycle management practices. Next, we explore the intricacies of managing CA hierarchies and key lifecycle, including CLI commands and deployment techniques, to ensure the integrity, availability, and security of PKI infrastructure.

Understanding CA Hierarchy: A CA hierarchy consists of multiple CAs organized in a hierarchical structure to facilitate certificate issuance, validation, and trust establishment. The hierarchy typically includes root CAs, intermediate CAs, and issuing CAs, each serving specific roles in the PKI ecosystem. Root CAs are self-signed and establish the trust anchor for the entire hierarchy, while intermediate CAs and issuing CAs are subordinate to root CAs and issue certificates on their behalf.

Planning CA Hierarchy: Before deploying CA hierarchy, organizations must define the hierarchy structure, determine the number of CAs needed, and establish trust relationships between CAs. Key considerations include:

Root CA Placement: Decide whether to deploy a single root CA or multiple root CAs based on scalability, fault tolerance, and regulatory requirements. Consider factors such as geographic distribution, organizational structure, and security posture when planning root CA deployment.

Intermediate CAs: Determine the number and placement of intermediate CAs to balance certificate issuance workload, enhance scalability, and facilitate certificate chain validation. Deploy intermediate CAs in separate security zones or administrative domains to isolate risks and enforce separation of duties.

Issuing CAs: Define issuing CAs responsible for issuing certificates to end entities, such as users, computers, and devices. Configure issuing CAs with specific certificate templates, enrollment policies, and certificate revocation mechanisms based on application requirements and security policies.

Deploying CA Hierarchy: Deploying CA hierarchy involves installing and configuring root CAs, intermediate CAs, and issuing CAs, establishing trust relationships between CAs, and securing private keys. Here are some CLI commands and techniques for deploying CA hierarchy:

Install Root CA:

```
mathematicaCopy code
Install-WindowsFeature -Name ADCS-Cert-Authority
```

Install Intermediate CA:

```
sqlCopy code
Add-WindowsFeature ADCS-Cert-Authority
```

Configure Trust Relationship:

```
arduinoCopy code
certutil -addstore -f "Root" RootCA.crt
```

Secure Private Keys:

```
perlCopy code
certutil -repairstore my "SerialNumber"
```

Key Lifecycle Management: Key lifecycle management involves generating, renewing, and revoking cryptographic keys and certificates to maintain the security and integrity of the PKI infrastructure. Key lifecycle management practices include:

Key Generation: Generate cryptographic keys using secure algorithms and key lengths appropriate for the intended use case. Use tools such as OpenSSL or Microsoft Certificate Services to generate key pairs and certificate signing requests (CSRs) for CAs and end entities.

Certificate Renewal: Renew certificates before they expire to ensure uninterrupted service and prevent certificate expiration issues. Implement certificate renewal policies, automate certificate renewal processes, and monitor certificate expiration dates to avoid service disruptions.

Certificate Revocation: Revoke certificates promptly when compromised, lost, or no longer needed to prevent unauthorized use and maintain trust within the PKI ecosystem. Use certificate revocation mechanisms such as Certificate Revocation Lists (CRLs) or Online Certificate Status Protocol (OCSP) to publish revocation information and notify relying parties.

Key Backup and Recovery: Implement key backup and recovery procedures to protect against data loss or corruption due to hardware failures, software errors, or malicious attacks. Use key archival mechanisms, offline key backups, and key escrow services to securely store private keys and recovery materials.

Monitoring and Auditing: Regular monitoring and auditing of CA hierarchy and key lifecycle activities are essential for detecting security incidents, compliance violations, or operational issues. Monitoring and auditing practices include:

Event Logging: Monitor CA events, audit logs, and performance counters to track certificate issuance, renewal, revocation, and key management activities. Use tools such as Event Viewer, PowerShell scripts, or centralized logging solutions to capture and analyze CA-related events.

Auditing Compliance: Conduct periodic audits and assessments of CA hierarchy and key lifecycle processes to ensure compliance with organizational policies, industry standards, and regulatory requirements. Verify adherence to security controls, encryption algorithms, key management practices, and certificate issuance policies.

Incident Response: Establish incident response procedures for handling security breaches, certificate compromises, or key management incidents. Define roles and responsibilities, escalation procedures, and mitigation strategies to respond effectively to security incidents and minimize impact on PKI operations.

Managing certificate authority hierarchies and key lifecycle is critical for maintaining the security, integrity, and availability of PKI infrastructure. By following best practices, leveraging CLI commands and deployment techniques, and implementing robust key lifecycle management processes, organizations can establish a resilient CA hierarchy, protect sensitive cryptographic assets, and ensure the trustworthiness of digital certificates issued within their PKI ecosystem.

Chapter 8: Active Directory Rights Management Services (AD RMS)

Active Directory Rights Management Services (AD RMS) is a server role in Windows Server that provides information protection capabilities by encrypting and restricting access to sensitive documents and emails. Deploying and configuring AD RMS involves setting up server roles, configuring policies, and integrating with applications to protect confidential data. Next, we explore the process of deploying and configuring AD RMS, including CLI commands and deployment techniques, to safeguard sensitive information within organizations.

Understanding AD RMS: AD RMS enables organizations to create and enforce information protection policies for documents and emails. It uses encryption, rights management, and policy enforcement to control access to protected content and prevent unauthorized disclosure or misuse of sensitive information. AD RMS integrates with applications such as Microsoft Office, SharePoint, and Exchange to provide seamless information protection capabilities.

Planning AD RMS Deployment: Before deploying AD RMS, organizations must assess their information protection requirements and plan the deployment strategy. Key considerations include:

Scope of Protection: Define the types of content and scenarios that require protection, such as confidential documents, intellectual property, or sensitive emails. Determine the scope of protection, including user groups, departments, or business units that require access to protected content.

Integration with Applications: Identify the applications and services that will integrate with AD RMS for information protection. Evaluate compatibility with existing infrastructure, such as Office applications, SharePoint document libraries, and Exchange mailboxes, to ensure seamless integration and user experience.

Infrastructure Design: Design the AD RMS infrastructure for scalability, availability, and performance. Decide whether to deploy a single-server or multi-server configuration, select hardware and software requirements, and plan for redundancy, disaster recovery, and high availability.

Deploying AD RMS: Deploying AD RMS involves installing server roles, configuring server settings, and integrating with directory services. Here are some CLI commands and techniques for deploying AD RMS:

Install AD RMS Server Role:

mathematicaCopy code

```
Install-WindowsFeature -Name ADRMS
```

Configure AD RMS Server:

mathematicaCopy code

```
Initialize-ADRMS -Verbose
```

Configure AD RMS Cluster:

mathematicaCopy code

```
Initialize-ADRMS -Cluster
```

Activate AD RMS Server:

mathematicaCopy code

```
Initialize-ADRMS -Activate -Verbose
```

Register SCP in Active Directory:

mathematicaCopy code

```
Initialize-ADRMS -RegisterSCP
```

Configuring AD RMS Policies: Configuring AD RMS policies involves defining usage rights, encryption settings, and access controls for protected content. Here are some configuration tasks:

Define Usage Rights: Create usage policy templates to specify permissions, such as view, edit, print, and copy, for protected content. Customize usage rights based on user roles, organizational requirements, and compliance regulations.

Configure Encryption Settings: Specify encryption algorithms, key lengths, and cryptographic parameters for encrypting protected content. Choose encryption options that balance security requirements with performance and compatibility considerations.

Set Expiration and Revocation Policies: Define expiration dates and revocation policies for protected content to enforce data retention policies and mitigate risks associated with unauthorized access or misuse. Configure expiration rules, automatic revocation triggers, and auditing mechanisms to track content lifecycle events.

Integrating with Applications: Integrating AD RMS with applications enables seamless information protection and rights management within familiar user interfaces. Here are integration tasks:

Configure Office Integration: Enable AD RMS protection features in Microsoft Office applications, such as Word, Excel, PowerPoint, and Outlook, to allow users to apply protection policies directly from the application ribbon.

Integrate with SharePoint: Configure AD RMS protection for SharePoint document libraries to enforce access controls, encryption, and usage rights for documents stored in SharePoint sites. Enable document-level protection and collaboration features for SharePoint users.

Integrate with Exchange: Enable AD RMS protection for email messages and attachments in Exchange mailboxes to prevent data leakage and unauthorized access. Configure transport rules, message classifications, and encryption settings for Exchange Online or Exchange Server deployments.

Monitoring and Auditing: Regular monitoring and auditing of AD RMS activities is essential for detecting security incidents, compliance violations, or operational issues. Monitoring and auditing practices include:

Event Logging: Monitor AD RMS events, audit logs, and performance counters to track information protection activities, policy enforcement events, and user interactions with protected content. Use tools such as Event Viewer, PowerShell scripts, or centralized logging solutions to capture and analyze AD RMS events.

Auditing Compliance: Conduct periodic audits and assessments of AD RMS configuration settings, policy templates, and usage reports to ensure compliance with organizational policies, industry standards, and regulatory requirements. Verify adherence to encryption standards, access controls, and data protection policies.

Incident Response: Establish incident response procedures for handling security breaches, policy violations, or user errors related to information protection. Define roles and responsibilities, escalation procedures, and mitigation strategies to respond effectively to security incidents and minimize impact on data confidentiality and integrity.

Deploying and configuring Active Directory Rights Management Services (AD RMS) is critical for protecting sensitive information and enforcing information protection policies within organizations. By following best practices, leveraging CLI commands and deployment techniques, and integrating with applications, organizations can establish a robust information protection framework that safeguards confidential data, mitigates risks, and ensures compliance with regulatory requirements.

Integrating Active Directory Rights Management Services (AD RMS) with Document Management Systems (DMS) enhances information protection and access control capabilities, allowing organizations to secure sensitive documents, control document permissions, and enforce compliance policies. Next, we explore the process of integrating AD RMS with DMS, including CLI commands and deployment techniques, to enable seamless information protection within document-centric workflows.

Understanding AD RMS Integration: AD RMS integration with DMS platforms enables organizations to extend information protection policies to documents stored within document repositories, collaboration platforms, and content management systems. By integrating AD RMS with DMS, organizations can apply granular access controls, encryption, and usage policies to protect documents from unauthorized access, sharing, or modification.

Planning AD RMS Integration: Before integrating AD RMS with DMS, organizations must assess their document management requirements, evaluate DMS compatibility with AD RMS, and define integration objectives. Key considerations include:

DMS Selection: Choose a DMS platform that supports AD RMS integration and provides seamless integration capabilities, such as native support for AD RMS protection features, integration APIs, or custom extensions for information protection.

Integration Scenarios: Define integration scenarios based on document lifecycle stages, user workflows, and business processes. Determine how AD RMS protection policies will be applied to documents, including encryption, access controls, usage rights, and document expiration settings.

User Experience: Consider the impact of AD RMS integration on user experience within the DMS platform. Ensure that users can apply AD RMS protection directly from the DMS interface, view protected documents, and collaborate securely without disrupting productivity.

Deploying AD RMS Integration: Deploying AD RMS integration with DMS involves configuring AD RMS server settings, enabling DMS integration features, and configuring document protection settings. Here are some CLI commands and techniques for deploying AD RMS integration:

Enable RMS Sharing in Office 365:

pythonCopy code

```
Set-IRMConfiguration -RMSOnlineKeySharingLocation "https://sp-rms.na.aadrm.com/TenantManagement/ServicePartner.svc" -InternalLicensingEnabled $True
```

Configure RMS Connector for SharePoint:

javascriptCopy code

Set-IRMConfiguration -RMSOnlineConnectionString "https://sp-rms.na.aadrm.com/_wmcs/licensing" -LicensingLocation "https://sp-rms.na.aadrm.com/_wmcs/licensing"

Enable RMS Protection for Exchange Online:

pythonCopy code

Set-IRMConfiguration -InternalLicensingEnabled $True

Configure RMS Protection for SharePoint Online:

pythonCopy code

Set-IRMConfiguration -SimplifiedClientAccessEnabled $True

Configuring DMS Integration: Configuring DMS integration with AD RMS involves enabling RMS protection features, configuring document libraries or repositories for AD RMS protection, and defining document protection policies. Here are configuration tasks:

Enable RMS Protection Features: Enable RMS protection features within the DMS platform, such as SharePoint, OneDrive, or third-party DMS solutions. Configure integration settings, RMS connector URLs, and authentication options to enable seamless RMS protection.

Configure Document Libraries: Configure document libraries, folders, or repositories within the DMS platform for AD RMS protection. Define document-level protection settings, such as default protection templates, custom protection policies, and encryption options.

Apply AD RMS Protection: Apply AD RMS protection to individual documents or document libraries within the DMS platform. Enable users to apply protection policies directly from the DMS interface, specify access controls, usage rights, and expiration settings, and track document usage with audit logs.

User Experience and Collaboration: AD RMS integration with DMS platforms enhances user experience and enables secure collaboration within document-centric workflows. Here are user experience enhancements:

Seamless Protection: Enable users to apply AD RMS protection directly from the DMS interface, using familiar workflows and controls. Provide options for applying protection templates, specifying access permissions, and revoking access to protected documents.

Document Sharing: Facilitate secure document sharing and collaboration within the DMS platform. Allow users to share protected documents with internal and external collaborators, track document access and usage, and enforce protection policies across shared documents.

Mobile Access: Ensure compatibility with mobile devices and platforms, enabling users to access protected documents from smartphones, tablets, and other mobile devices. Provide mobile apps or web interfaces for viewing, editing, and sharing protected documents securely on the go.

Monitoring and Auditing: Regular monitoring and auditing of AD RMS integration with DMS platforms are essential for detecting security incidents, compliance violations, or operational issues. Monitoring and auditing practices include:

Audit Logs: Monitor AD RMS audit logs, DMS activity logs, and user access logs to track document protection events, user interactions, and policy enforcement activities. Use logging and monitoring tools to capture and analyze audit data, detect anomalies, and investigate security incidents.

Compliance Reporting: Generate compliance reports and audit trails to demonstrate adherence to information protection policies, regulatory requirements, and industry standards. Provide visibility into document usage, access patterns, and compliance violations to stakeholders, auditors, and regulatory authorities.

Incident Response: Establish incident response procedures for handling security breaches, unauthorized access attempts, or policy violations related to AD RMS integration with DMS platforms. Define roles and responsibilities, escalation procedures, and mitigation strategies to respond effectively to security incidents and minimize impact on data confidentiality and integrity.

Integrating Active Directory Rights Management Services (AD RMS) with Document Management Systems (DMS) enhances information protection capabilities, enabling organizations to secure sensitive documents, control access, and enforce compliance policies within document-centric workflows. By following best practices, leveraging CLI commands and deployment techniques, and prioritizing user experience and collaboration, organizations can establish a robust information protection framework that safeguards confidential data, facilitates secure collaboration, and ensures compliance with regulatory requirements.

Chapter 9: Active Directory Disaster Recovery and High Availability

Active Directory (AD) serves as the backbone of Windows-based network environments, storing critical information such as user accounts, group policies, and domain configurations. Implementing effective backup and restore strategies for Active Directory is essential to ensure data integrity, minimize downtime, and recover from disasters efficiently. Next, we delve into the intricacies of Active Directory backup and restore strategies, including CLI commands and deployment techniques, to help organizations safeguard their directory service infrastructure.

Understanding Active Directory Backup and Restore: Active Directory backup involves creating copies of AD database files (NTDS.dit) and associated system state data, while restore refers to the process of recovering AD objects, configurations, and attributes from backup copies. A robust backup and restore strategy encompasses regular backups, secure storage, testing restore procedures, and maintaining backup integrity.

Planning Backup and Restore: Before implementing backup and restore strategies for Active Directory, organizations must assess their business continuity requirements, define recovery point objectives (RPOs) and recovery time objectives (RTOs), and evaluate available backup solutions. Key considerations include:

Backup Frequency: Determine the frequency of AD backups based on data volatility, change rate, and business requirements. Consider daily, weekly, or incremental backups to capture changes and minimize data loss in case of failures.

Retention Policies: Define retention policies for backup data, specifying how long backup copies should be retained and whether they should be archived or deleted after a certain period. Align retention policies with compliance regulations, data protection laws, and organizational data management policies.

Backup Storage: Select appropriate storage solutions for storing AD backup data, such as on-premises disk storage, network-attached storage (NAS), tape drives, or cloud storage. Ensure data integrity, encryption, and redundancy to protect backup copies from corruption, unauthorized access, or hardware failures.

Deploying Backup Solutions: Deploying backup solutions for Active Directory involves selecting backup software, configuring backup schedules, and testing backup and restore procedures. Here are some CLI commands and techniques for deploying backup solutions:

Windows Server Backup (WSB):

phpCopy code

```
wbadmin start systemstatebackup -backuptarget:<TargetVolume>
```

Third-Party Backup Solutions:

cssCopy code

```
VeeamBackup.exe --backup "Domain Controllers" --target <BackupLocation>
```

Azure Backup:

sqlCopy code

```
New-AzRecoveryServicesBackupProtectionPolicy -Name "AD Backup Policy" -WorkloadType "AzureVM" -BackupManagementType "AzureVM"
```

Configuring Backup Settings: Configure backup settings to specify what data to include in AD backups, how often backups should occur, and where backup copies should be stored. Here are configuration tasks:

System State Backup: Include System State data in AD backups to capture critical components such as registry settings, boot files, and AD database files (NTDS.dit).

Backup Schedule: Define backup schedules to automate backup tasks and ensure consistency across backup operations. Schedule full, incremental, or differential backups based on backup policies and data protection requirements.

Backup Retention: Configure backup retention settings to specify how long backup copies should be retained and whether they should be archived or deleted after a certain period.

Testing Restore Procedures: Regularly test restore procedures to validate backup integrity, verify recovery capabilities, and ensure readiness for disaster recovery scenarios. Here are testing procedures:

Test Restores: Perform test restores of AD backups in a non-production environment to verify backup integrity, data consistency, and recoverability. Use testing tools, virtualization platforms, or isolated test environments to simulate restore scenarios and assess recovery outcomes.

Recovery Point Validation: Validate recovery points by comparing backup data with production data to ensure data consistency, accuracy, and completeness. Use checksums, hash values, or file-level comparisons to verify backup integrity and detect any discrepancies or data corruption.

Disaster Recovery Drills: Conduct disaster recovery drills to assess readiness, evaluate response procedures, and train IT staff on recovery tasks. Simulate disaster scenarios, such as server failures, data corruption, or ransomware attacks, and practice recovery procedures to minimize downtime and data loss.

Monitoring and Auditing: Regular monitoring and auditing of backup operations are essential for detecting issues, ensuring compliance, and maintaining backup integrity. Monitoring and auditing practices include:

Backup Logs: Monitor backup logs, event logs, and backup status reports to track backup operations, identify errors or warnings, and troubleshoot issues. Use monitoring tools, log analysis software, or centralized logging solutions to capture and analyze backup logs.

Backup Verification: Verify backup integrity and data consistency by comparing backup copies with production data, performing data validation checks, and monitoring backup success rates. Use verification tools, data validation scripts, or checksum algorithms to ensure backup reliability and accuracy.

Compliance Reporting: Generate compliance reports and audit trails to demonstrate adherence to backup policies, regulatory requirements, and industry standards. Provide visibility into backup activities, retention policies, and data protection controls to stakeholders, auditors, and regulatory authorities.

Ensuring high availability (HA) for Active Directory (AD) is crucial for maintaining uninterrupted access to directory services and minimizing downtime in enterprise environments. High availability solutions for AD involve deploying redundant domain controllers, implementing fault-tolerant replication mechanisms, and configuring disaster recovery strategies. Next, we explore various techniques, CLI commands, and best practices for configuring Active Directory high availability solutions to enhance resilience and reliability.

Understanding Active Directory High Availability: Active Directory high availability refers to the ability of the AD infrastructure to withstand failures, maintain service availability, and ensure data integrity even in the event of hardware failures, software glitches, or network outages. HA solutions aim to eliminate single points of failure, distribute workload across multiple domain controllers, and provide seamless failover capabilities to minimize service disruptions.

Planning for High Availability: Before implementing high availability solutions for Active Directory, organizations must conduct a thorough assessment of their business requirements, infrastructure topology, and service level objectives (SLOs). Key considerations include:

Redundancy Requirements: Determine the level of redundancy needed for domain controllers, global catalog servers, and DNS infrastructure to achieve desired levels of availability and fault tolerance.

Site Topology: Analyze the AD site topology, network connectivity, and replication topology to identify potential bottlenecks, latency issues, and points of failure. Design site links, bridgehead servers, and replication schedules to optimize AD replication and ensure timely data synchronization.

Disaster Recovery Planning: Develop disaster recovery plans, backup and restore procedures, and failover strategies to mitigate risks associated with hardware failures, data corruption, or catastrophic events. Define roles and responsibilities, establish communication channels, and conduct regular drills to test recovery procedures and validate readiness.

Deploying Redundant Domain Controllers: Deploying redundant domain controllers is the cornerstone of Active Directory high availability. Redundant domain controllers ensure that authentication requests, directory queries, and group policy updates remain available even if one or more domain controllers fail. Here are some CLI commands and techniques for deploying redundant domain controllers:

Promote Additional Domain Controller:

rubyCopy code

```
dcpromo    /unattend    /replicaOrNewDomain:replica
/replicaDomainDNSName:<DomainDNSName>
/DatabasePath:<DatabasePath>    /LogPath:<LogPath>
/SYSVOLPath:<SYSVOLPath>
```

Install Additional Domain Controller with PowerShell:

phpCopy code

```
Install-ADDSDomainController    -DomainName
<DomainName> -SiteName <SiteName> -InstallDns -Force -
NoRebootOnCompletion
```

Create Additional Global Catalog Server:

mathematicaCopy code

```
Get-ADForest    |    Set-ADForest    -GlobalCatalogs
<GlobalCatalogServers>
```

Configuring Active Directory Sites and Services: Active Directory Sites and Services (ADSS) is a management console used to configure AD site topology, site links, and replication settings. Configuring ADSS is essential for optimizing AD replication, minimizing replication latency, and ensuring efficient failover in multi-site environments. Here are some configuration tasks:

Create AD Sites: Define Active Directory sites to represent physical locations, network segments, or administrative boundaries within the organization. Associate domain controllers with appropriate sites based on proximity, network connectivity, and site link configuration.

Configure Site Links: Create site links to establish replication connections between AD sites and control the flow of replication traffic. Specify costs, replication intervals, and replication schedules for site links to optimize replication performance and bandwidth utilization.

Designate Bridgehead Servers: Designate bridgehead servers to serve as replication endpoints between sites and facilitate intersite replication traffic. Distribute bridgehead servers evenly across sites, ensure sufficient hardware resources, and monitor replication queues to detect bottlenecks or performance issues.

Implementing DNS High Availability: DNS is a critical component of Active Directory infrastructure, providing name resolution services for domain controllers, clients, and applications. Implementing DNS high availability involves deploying redundant DNS servers, configuring DNS replication, and optimizing DNS resolution. Here are some techniques:

Deploy DNS Round Robin: Configure DNS round-robin load balancing to distribute DNS queries across multiple DNS servers and enhance fault tolerance. Create multiple DNS A records with the same hostname but different IP addresses to achieve load distribution and redundancy.

Configure DNS Zone Transfers: Enable DNS zone transfers between primary and secondary DNS servers to synchronize DNS zone data and ensure consistency across DNS servers. Configure zone transfer settings, access control lists (ACLs), and notification mechanisms to secure zone transfers and prevent unauthorized access.

Implement DNS Anycast: Deploy DNS anycast routing to provide redundancy and fault tolerance for DNS resolution. Configure multiple DNS servers with the same IP address and advertise the IP address via multiple network routes to distribute DNS queries to the nearest available server.

Monitoring and Maintenance: Regular monitoring and maintenance of Active Directory high availability solutions are essential for detecting issues, optimizing performance, and ensuring continuous service availability. Here are some monitoring and maintenance tasks:

Monitor Replication Status: Monitor AD replication status, replication latency, and replication errors using tools such as Repadmin, Active Directory Replication Status Tool (ADREPLSTATUS), or PowerShell cmdlets. Analyze replication topology, event logs, and replication metadata to identify replication issues and troubleshoot replication errors.

Perform Health Checks: Perform regular health checks of domain controllers, DNS servers, and network infrastructure to detect hardware failures, software issues, or configuration errors. Use performance monitoring tools, system logs, and diagnostic utilities to assess system health, identify performance bottlenecks, and preempt potential failures.

Patch Management: Implement a patch management strategy to keep domain controllers, DNS servers, and operating systems up to date with the latest security updates, hotfixes, and service packs. Schedule regular patching cycles, test patches in a non-production environment, and follow best practices for patch deployment to minimize service disruptions and security vulnerabilities.

Configuring Active Directory high availability solutions is essential for maintaining uninterrupted access to directory services, minimizing downtime, and ensuring business continuity. By deploying redundant domain controllers, optimizing AD site topology, and implementing DNS high availability, organizations can enhance resilience, reliability, and fault tolerance in their AD infrastructure. With proper planning, deployment, and monitoring, organizations can mitigate risks associated with hardware failures, network outages, or software glitches, and provide seamless access to critical directory services for users and applications.

Chapter 10: Active Directory Integration with Cloud Services

Integrating on-premises Active Directory (AD) with Azure Active Directory (AAD) provides organizations with a hybrid identity solution, enabling seamless authentication and access control across on-premises and cloud-based resources. This integration allows users to use a single set of credentials to access both local network resources and cloud-based applications, enhancing security, simplifying identity management, and streamlining access control. Next, we explore the process of integrating Active Directory with Azure Active Directory, including CLI commands and deployment techniques, to help organizations establish a unified identity infrastructure.

Understanding Azure Active Directory (AAD): Azure Active Directory is Microsoft's cloud-based identity and access management service, providing authentication, authorization, and identity protection for cloud-based applications and services. AAD acts as a comprehensive identity platform, offering features such as single sign-on (SSO), multi-factor authentication (MFA), conditional access policies, and identity governance.

Benefits of Integrating AD with AAD: Integrating on-premises Active Directory with Azure Active Directory offers several benefits:

Unified Identity Management: Centralize identity management across on-premises and cloud environments, allowing users to access resources seamlessly using a single set of credentials.

Single Sign-On (SSO): Enable users to sign in once with their corporate credentials and access both on-premises and cloud-based applications without having to re-enter credentials.

Enhanced Security: Implement advanced security features such as multi-factor authentication (MFA), conditional access policies, and identity protection to safeguard against unauthorized access and identity-based threats.

Streamlined Access Control: Define access policies and permissions centrally in Active Directory and enforce them consistently across on-premises and cloud environments, ensuring compliance and reducing administrative overhead.

Preparing Active Directory for Integration: Before integrating Active Directory with Azure Active Directory, ensure that the on-premises AD environment meets the prerequisites and requirements for synchronization. Key preparatory steps include:

Active Directory Cleanup: Clean up and consolidate Active Directory objects, remove duplicate or obsolete accounts, and ensure that user attributes are accurate and up to date.

DNS Configuration: Verify DNS configuration and ensure that domain controllers can resolve Azure AD endpoints and connect to the Azure AD service.

Firewall Configuration: Configure firewall rules to allow outbound communication from domain controllers to Azure AD endpoints over the required ports and protocols (e.g., TCP port 443).

Deploying Azure AD Connect: Azure AD Connect is the tool used to synchronize on-premises Active Directory with Azure Active Directory. It enables directory synchronization, password hash synchronization, and seamless single sign-on. Here are the deployment steps:

Download and Install Azure AD Connect: Download the Azure AD Connect tool from the Microsoft website and install it on a dedicated server in the on-premises environment.

Configure Synchronization Options: During installation, configure synchronization options such as the synchronization scope, filtering options, and synchronization frequency based on organizational requirements.

Specify Azure AD Credentials: Provide Azure AD credentials and establish a trust relationship between the on-premises AD forest and Azure AD.

Enable Password Hash Synchronization (PHS): Optionally, enable password hash synchronization to synchronize on-premises user passwords with Azure AD, allowing users to sign in to cloud services using their on-premises passwords.

Enable Seamless Single Sign-On (SSO): Optionally, configure seamless single sign-on to enable users to authenticate to cloud services using their on-premises credentials without having to enter their passwords again.

Monitoring and Managing Synchronization: After deploying Azure AD Connect, it's essential to monitor synchronization status, troubleshoot any synchronization errors, and manage the synchronization process effectively. Here are some monitoring and management tasks:

Monitoring Synchronization Status: Use the Azure AD Connect Health dashboard to monitor synchronization status, review synchronization errors, and track overall health and performance.

Troubleshooting Synchronization Errors: Investigate synchronization errors, identify root causes, and resolve issues promptly to ensure uninterrupted synchronization between on-premises AD and Azure AD.

Managing Attribute Mapping: Customize attribute mapping rules to ensure accurate synchronization of user attributes, group memberships, and other directory objects between on-premises AD and Azure AD.

Implementing Conditional Access Policies: Azure AD conditional access policies allow organizations to enforce access controls based on various conditions such as user identity, device compliance, location, and risk level. Implementing conditional access policies enhances security and ensures that access to resources is granted based on contextual factors. Here's how to implement conditional access policies:

Define Access Policies: Define conditional access policies based on organizational security requirements, compliance regulations, and risk assessments. Specify conditions, access controls, and enforcement actions for different scenarios.

Enable Multi-Factor Authentication (MFA): Require multi-factor authentication for specific users, groups, or applications to add an extra layer of security and mitigate the risk of unauthorized access.

Implement Device Compliance Checks: Verify device compliance before granting access to resources by enforcing device-based access policies and requiring devices to meet specified security and compliance standards.

Integrating Active Directory with Azure Active Directory enables organizations to establish a unified identity infrastructure, providing seamless authentication, access control, and identity management across on-premises and cloud environments. By deploying Azure AD Connect, configuring synchronization options, and implementing conditional access policies, organizations can enhance security, streamline access control, and ensure a consistent user experience while leveraging the benefits of cloud-based identity services. With proper planning, deployment, and management, organizations can maximize the value of their hybrid identity solutions and enable secure, productive collaboration in today's interconnected digital landscape.

Hybrid identity solutions with Microsoft 365 offer organizations the flexibility to leverage both on-premises Active Directory (AD) and cloud-based Azure Active Directory

(AAD) services, enabling seamless authentication, access control, and identity management across hybrid environments. By integrating on-premises AD with Microsoft 365, organizations can achieve a unified identity infrastructure, enhance security, and facilitate productivity for users accessing cloud-based services. Next, we explore the process of implementing hybrid identity solutions with Microsoft 365, including CLI commands and deployment techniques, to help organizations establish a cohesive identity management strategy.

Understanding Hybrid Identity Solutions: Hybrid identity solutions bridge the gap between on-premises and cloud-based identity services, allowing organizations to extend their existing on-premises identity infrastructure to the cloud. By integrating on-premises AD with Microsoft 365, users can authenticate seamlessly across both environments, access cloud-based resources with their existing credentials, and benefit from centralized identity management.

Benefits of Hybrid Identity Solutions: Implementing hybrid identity solutions with Microsoft 365 offers several benefits:

Unified Identity Management: Centralize identity management across on-premises and cloud environments, providing users with a single set of credentials for authentication and access control.

Enhanced Security: Strengthen security posture by enforcing consistent identity policies, implementing multi-factor authentication (MFA), and monitoring user access across hybrid environments.

Seamless Access to Cloud Services: Enable users to access cloud-based services such as Microsoft 365, Azure services, and third-party applications using their on-premises credentials, enhancing productivity and user experience.

Simplified Administration: Streamline identity administration tasks by managing user accounts, group memberships, and access policies from a centralized console, reducing administrative overhead and complexity.

Preparing for Hybrid Identity Integration: Before integrating on-premises AD with Microsoft 365, organizations must prepare their existing infrastructure and meet certain prerequisites. Key preparatory steps include:

Assessing Infrastructure Readiness: Evaluate the existing on-premises AD environment, domain controller infrastructure, and network connectivity to ensure compatibility with Microsoft 365 services.

Verifying Domain Ownership: Verify domain ownership and configure DNS records to establish trust between on-premises AD and Microsoft 365, enabling seamless authentication and directory synchronization.

Ensuring Security Compliance: Review security policies, access controls, and compliance requirements to ensure that data protection and regulatory standards are met when extending identity services to the cloud.

Deploying Azure AD Connect for Directory Synchronization: Azure AD Connect is the primary tool used to synchronize on-premises AD with Azure Active Directory. It enables directory synchronization, password hash synchronization, and seamless single sign-on (SSO) capabilities. Here's how to deploy Azure AD Connect:

Download and Install Azure AD Connect: Download the Azure AD Connect tool from the Microsoft website and install it on a dedicated server within the on-premises environment.

Configure Synchronization Options: During installation, configure synchronization options such as the synchronization scope, filtering options, and synchronization frequency based on organizational requirements.

Specify Azure AD Credentials: Provide Azure AD credentials and establish a trust relationship between the on-premises AD forest and Azure AD, allowing for secure synchronization of directory objects.

Enable Password Hash Synchronization (PHS): Optionally, enable password hash synchronization to synchronize on-premises user passwords with Azure AD, enabling users to sign in to cloud services using their on-premises passwords.

Enable Seamless Single Sign-On (SSO): Optionally, configure seamless SSO to enable users to authenticate to Microsoft 365 services using their on-premises credentials without having to enter their passwords again.

Implementing Conditional Access Policies: Azure AD conditional access policies allow organizations to enforce access controls based on various conditions such as user identity, device compliance, location, and risk level. Implementing conditional access policies enhances security and ensures that access to resources is granted based on contextual factors. Here's how to implement conditional access policies:

Define Access Policies: Define conditional access policies based on organizational security requirements, compliance regulations, and risk assessments. Specify conditions, access controls, and enforcement actions for different scenarios.

Enable Multi-Factor Authentication (MFA): Require multi-factor authentication for specific users, groups, or applications to add an extra layer of security and mitigate the risk of unauthorized access.

Implement Device Compliance Checks: Verify device compliance before granting access to resources by enforcing device-based access policies and requiring devices to meet specified security and compliance standards.

Monitoring and Managing Hybrid Identity Solutions: After deploying Azure AD Connect and implementing hybrid identity solutions, it's essential to monitor synchronization status, troubleshoot any synchronization errors, and manage access controls effectively. Here are some monitoring and management tasks:

Monitoring Synchronization Status: Use the Azure AD Connect Health dashboard to monitor synchronization status, review synchronization errors, and track overall health and performance.

Troubleshooting Synchronization Errors: Investigate synchronization errors, identify root causes, and resolve issues promptly to ensure uninterrupted synchronization between on-premises AD and Azure AD.

Managing Conditional Access Policies: Regularly review and update conditional access policies based on evolving security requirements, user feedback, and changes in organizational policies to maintain an effective access control framework.

Implementing hybrid identity solutions with Microsoft 365 enables organizations to extend their existing on-premises identity infrastructure to the cloud, providing users with seamless access to cloud-based services while maintaining centralized identity management. By deploying Azure AD Connect, configuring synchronization options, implementing conditional access policies, and monitoring hybrid identity solutions, organizations can enhance security, streamline access control, and ensure a consistent user experience across hybrid environments. With proper planning, deployment, and management, organizations can maximize the benefits of hybrid identity solutions and enable secure, productive collaboration in today's interconnected digital landscape.

BOOK 3
SECURING ACTIVE DIRECTORY
STRATEGIES AND BEST PRACTICES FOR IT SECURITY
PROFESSIONALS

ROB BOTWRIGHT

Chapter 1: Introduction to Active Directory Security

Active Directory (AD) serves as the cornerstone of identity and access management for most organizations, providing a centralized directory service for authentication, authorization, and resource management. However, despite its critical role, Active Directory is not immune to security risks and vulnerabilities. Understanding these risks is essential for organizations to implement effective security measures and safeguard their directory services against potential threats. Next, we delve into various security risks associated with Active Directory, explore common attack vectors, and discuss strategies for mitigating these risks.

Overview of Active Directory Security Risks: Active Directory faces a range of security risks, including insider threats, external attacks, misconfigurations, and vulnerabilities. These risks can result in unauthorized access to sensitive data, privilege escalation, data breaches, and service disruptions, posing significant threats to organizational security and compliance.

Common Active Directory Security Risks: Several factors contribute to Active Directory security risks, including:

Weak Passwords: Weak, easily guessable passwords pose a significant security risk, as they can be exploited by attackers to gain unauthorized access to user accounts, compromise sensitive data, or perform lateral movement within the network.

Unpatched Systems: Failure to apply security patches and updates to domain controllers, servers, and client systems leaves them vulnerable to known exploits and vulnerabilities, increasing the risk of compromise and exploitation.

Privilege Abuse: Insider threats, malicious insiders, or compromised accounts with excessive privileges can abuse their access rights to perform unauthorized actions, exfiltrate data, or disrupt operations, leading to security breaches and compliance violations.

Inadequate Access Controls: Poorly configured access controls, excessive permissions, and inconsistent enforcement of security policies can result in unauthorized access to sensitive resources, data leakage, and exposure of critical systems to unauthorized users.

Lack of Monitoring and Detection: Inadequate monitoring, logging, and alerting mechanisms make it difficult to detect suspicious activities, unauthorized access attempts, or security breaches in real-time, allowing attackers to operate undetected within the network.

Understanding Attack Vectors: Attackers employ various techniques and attack vectors to target Active Directory environments, including:

Password Attacks: Attackers use brute-force attacks, password spraying, or credential stuffing techniques to guess or compromise user passwords and gain unauthorized access to accounts.

Phishing and Social Engineering: Phishing emails, malicious links, or social engineering tactics are used to trick users into disclosing their credentials or installing malware, enabling attackers to compromise user accounts and access the network.

Exploiting Vulnerabilities: Attackers exploit known vulnerabilities in Active Directory components, operating systems, or third-party applications to gain unauthorized access, escalate privileges, or compromise the integrity of the directory service.

Lateral Movement: Once inside the network, attackers attempt to move laterally across systems, escalate privileges, and gain access to sensitive resources, leveraging compromised credentials or exploiting misconfigurations in AD.

Mitigating Active Directory Security Risks: To mitigate Active Directory security risks and enhance overall security posture, organizations should implement a comprehensive set of security controls and best practices, including:

Enforcing Strong Password Policies: Implement strong password policies, multi-factor authentication (MFA), and regular password rotation to prevent password-based attacks and unauthorized access.

Patch Management: Establish a robust patch management process to regularly update and patch domain controllers, servers, and endpoints with the latest security updates and fixes to mitigate known vulnerabilities.

Least Privilege Principle: Follow the principle of least privilege and enforce granular access controls to restrict user permissions and limit the scope of potential security breaches.

Monitoring and Logging: Implement robust monitoring, logging, and auditing mechanisms to track user activities, monitor privileged access, and detect anomalous behavior or security incidents in real-time.

Security Awareness Training: Provide regular security awareness training and education to users, administrators, and IT staff to raise awareness of common security risks, best practices, and incident response procedures.

Active Directory serves as a critical component of organizational infrastructure, centralizing identity and access management functions for users, devices, and resources. However, it also presents significant security risks and challenges, including insider threats, external attacks, and vulnerabilities. By understanding these risks, adopting proactive security measures, and implementing best practices for securing Active Directory, organizations can strengthen their defenses, mitigate potential threats, and safeguard their directory services against unauthorized access, data breaches, and security incidents. With a comprehensive approach to Active Directory security, organizations can enhance resilience, protect sensitive data, and maintain trust and integrity in their IT environments.

Active Directory (AD) is a critical component of the Windows ecosystem, providing centralized authentication, authorization, and management of resources in a networked environment. As organizations increasingly rely on AD to support their operations, ensuring the security of AD infrastructure becomes paramount. This chapter provides an overview of security principles in Active Directory, covering fundamental concepts, best practices, and tools to strengthen the security posture of AD environments.

Principles of Active Directory Security: Security in Active Directory revolves around several key principles:

Authentication: Ensuring that users and devices are who they claim to be through the validation of credentials, such as usernames and passwords.

Authorization: Granting or denying access to resources based on the permissions assigned to users or groups.

Confidentiality: Protecting sensitive information from unauthorized access or disclosure by encrypting data and controlling access to it.

Integrity: Maintaining the accuracy and consistency of data within the directory by preventing unauthorized modifications or tampering.

Availability: Ensuring that AD services and resources are accessible and functional when needed, minimizing downtime and disruptions.

Understanding Active Directory Security Components: Active Directory security is enforced through various components and mechanisms:

Authentication Protocols: Active Directory supports multiple authentication protocols, including Kerberos, NTLM, and LDAP, which authenticate users and services within the domain.

Access Control Lists (ACLs): ACLs define permissions on AD objects, such as users, groups, and organizational units (OUs), specifying who can perform operations and access resources.

Group Policies: Group Policies enforce security settings and configurations across AD domains, allowing administrators to manage user and computer configurations centrally.

Auditing and Logging: AD auditing enables the tracking and logging of events related to authentication, access control, and administrative activities, aiding in security monitoring and compliance.

Encryption and Secure Communication: Encrypting communication channels using protocols like Secure Sockets Layer (SSL) or Transport Layer Security (TLS) ensures the confidentiality and integrity of data exchanged between AD components.

Best Practices for Active Directory Security: Implementing robust security measures is essential to safeguarding Active Directory against threats and vulnerabilities. Key best practices include:

Implementing Least Privilege: Assign permissions and privileges on a need-to-know basis, granting users and groups only the permissions necessary to perform their roles.

Regular Patching and Updates: Keep AD servers and associated systems up-to-date with the latest security patches and updates to mitigate known vulnerabilities.

Enforcing Strong Password Policies: Implement policies requiring complex passwords, regular password changes, and multi-factor authentication to enhance authentication security.

Securing Administrative Access: Restrict administrative access to AD infrastructure, use separate administrative accounts, and employ techniques like Just Enough Administration (JEA) to limit privileges.

Monitoring and Auditing: Enable auditing of critical AD events, regularly review audit logs for suspicious activity, and implement real-time monitoring solutions to detect security incidents.

Tools for Active Directory Security: Several tools and utilities assist in securing Active Directory environments:

PowerShell: PowerShell commands (e.g., Get-ADUser, Set-ADGroup) enable administrators to perform various AD management tasks, including user management, group membership, and policy enforcement.

Group Policy Management Console (GPMC): GPMC provides a graphical interface for managing group policies, allowing administrators to configure security settings and deploy policies across the domain.

Security Configuration Wizard (SCW): SCW guides administrators through the process of securing Windows Server roles, including Active Directory Domain Services (AD DS), by applying recommended security settings.

Active Directory Administrative Center: ADAC offers a streamlined interface for managing AD objects and permissions, simplifying common administrative tasks and delegation.

Active Directory security is paramount for protecting organizational assets, ensuring compliance, and maintaining operational integrity. By adhering to security principles, implementing best practices, and leveraging appropriate tools, organizations can strengthen the security posture of their Active Directory environments and mitigate the risks associated with modern cyber threats. As threats evolve and security requirements change, continuous monitoring, assessment, and adaptation are crucial to maintaining a robust and resilient Active Directory infrastructure.

Chapter 2: Securing Active Directory Domain Controllers

Ensuring the security of an organization's Active Directory (AD) environment involves a multifaceted approach that encompasses both physical and logical security measures. Physical security focuses on safeguarding the physical infrastructure that houses AD servers and networking equipment, while logical security involves protecting the digital assets and data stored within the AD environment. This chapter explores various physical and logical security measures that organizations can implement to enhance the security posture of their AD infrastructure.

Physical Security Measures: Physical security measures are essential for protecting the hardware, facilities, and physical assets associated with the AD environment. Key physical security measures include:

Secure Access Controls: Limit physical access to server rooms, data centers, and network closets by implementing access controls such as badge readers, biometric scanners, and security guards. Use access logs to monitor and track entry and exit activity.

Surveillance Systems: Install surveillance cameras and monitoring systems to deter unauthorized access and record activities within sensitive areas. Regularly review surveillance footage to detect and investigate security incidents.

Environmental Controls: Maintain optimal environmental conditions, including temperature, humidity, and airflow, within server rooms and data centers to prevent hardware damage and ensure uninterrupted operation of AD servers and networking equipment.

Redundant Power and Connectivity: Implement redundant power supplies, uninterruptible power supplies (UPS), and network connections to mitigate the impact of power outages, equipment failures, or network disruptions on AD services.

Logical Security Measures: Logical security measures focus on securing the digital assets, data, and access controls within the AD environment. Key logical security measures include:

Strong Authentication Mechanisms: Enforce strong authentication mechanisms, including complex passwords, multi-factor authentication (MFA), and smart card authentication, to verify the identity of users accessing AD resources.

Access Controls and Permissions: Implement granular access controls and permissions to restrict user access to sensitive AD objects, such as domain controllers, organizational units (OUs), and group policies. Regularly review and audit permissions to ensure adherence to the principle of least privilege.

Encryption: Encrypt sensitive data transmitted between AD components, such as replication traffic between domain controllers, using protocols like Kerberos and SSL/TLS to prevent eavesdropping and data interception by unauthorized parties.

Auditing and Logging: Enable auditing and logging of AD events, including authentication attempts, privilege changes, and administrative activities, to track user actions, detect security incidents, and support forensic investigations.

Deploying Physical and Logical Security Measures: Deploying physical and logical security measures requires careful planning, implementation, and management. Here's how organizations can deploy these measures effectively:

Perform Risk Assessment: Conduct a comprehensive risk assessment to identify potential security threats, vulnerabilities, and risks associated with the AD environment, both physical and digital.

Develop Security Policies: Develop and document security policies and procedures that outline the requirements, guidelines, and responsibilities for implementing physical and logical security measures within the organization.

Implement Access Controls: Deploy access controls, such as firewalls, intrusion detection systems (IDS), and network segmentation, to protect the AD infrastructure from unauthorized access and network-based attacks.

Enforce Compliance Standards: Ensure compliance with relevant industry standards, regulations, and security frameworks, such as ISO 27001, NIST SP 800-53, and GDPR, to address legal and regulatory requirements for securing AD environments.

Regular Monitoring and Maintenance: Continuously monitor and maintain both physical and logical security measures, regularly reviewing access logs, conducting security audits, and performing vulnerability assessments to identify and remediate security gaps.

Implementing physical and logical security measures is essential for safeguarding an organization's Active Directory environment against a wide range of security threats and vulnerabilities. By combining robust physical security controls with effective logical security measures, organizations can mitigate the risk of unauthorized access, data breaches, and service disruptions, ensuring the confidentiality, integrity, and availability of AD resources. As security threats evolve and technologies advance, organizations must remain vigilant, adapt their security measures accordingly, and prioritize the protection of their AD infrastructure to maintain trust, compliance, and operational resilience.

Ensuring the security of domain controllers (DCs) is paramount in safeguarding the integrity and availability of an organization's Active Directory (AD) infrastructure. Domain controllers play a central role in authenticating users, authorizing access to resources, and maintaining the directory service's integrity. Therefore, hardening domain controller configuration settings is crucial to mitigate security risks and protect against potential threats. Next, we explore various techniques and best practices for hardening domain controller configuration settings to enhance the security posture of AD environments.

Understanding Domain Controller Security: Domain controllers serve as the primary point of authentication and authorization within an AD domain. As such, they are highly attractive targets for attackers seeking to compromise network security. Common security threats to domain controllers include unauthorized access, privilege escalation, denial of service attacks, and data exfiltration. Hardening domain controller configuration settings is essential to mitigate these risks and protect against potential security breaches.

Implementing Hardening Techniques: Hardening domain controller configuration involves implementing a series of security measures to reduce the attack surface and enhance resilience against security threats. Key techniques for hardening domain controller configuration settings include:

Enforcing Strong Password Policies: Set stringent password policies, including minimum password length, complexity requirements, and password expiration intervals, using Group Policy Objects (GPOs). Configure the "Password Policy" settings in the "Default Domain Policy" GPO using the Group Policy Management Console (GPMC) or PowerShell commands.

powershellCopy code

```
Set-ADDefaultDomainPasswordPolicy -ComplexityEnabled $true -MinimumPasswordLength 12 -MaxPasswordAge "90.00:00:00"
```

Disabling Unused Services and Features: Identify and disable unnecessary services and features on domain controllers to minimize the attack surface. Disable services such as Telnet, FTP, and SNMP, and remove unnecessary roles and features using the Server Manager or PowerShell.

powershellCopy code

```
Uninstall-WindowsFeature Telnet-Client, Telnet-Server
```

Implementing Network Segmentation: Use firewalls and network segmentation to restrict inbound and outbound traffic to domain controllers. Configure Windows Firewall rules to allow only necessary protocols and ports, such as LDAP, Kerberos, and DNS, and block all other traffic.

powershellCopy code

```
New-NetFirewallRule -DisplayName "Allow LDAP Inbound" -Direction Inbound -Protocol TCP -LocalPort 389 -Action Allow
```

Limiting Administrative Access: Restrict administrative access to domain controllers to authorized personnel only. Use the "Deny log on locally" and "Deny access to this computer from the network" user rights assignment settings in the "Default Domain Controllers Policy" GPO to prevent unauthorized access.

powershellCopy code

```
secedit /export /cfg C:\secconfig.cfg
```

Implementing Account Lockout Policies: Configure account lockout policies to prevent brute-force attacks and unauthorized access attempts. Set thresholds for account lockout duration, lockout threshold, and reset account lockout counter using GPOs.

powershellCopy code

```
Set-ADDefaultDomainPasswordPolicy -LockoutDuration "0.01:00:00" -LockoutThreshold 5 -ResetLockoutCount "0.00:30:00"
```

Performing Regular Security Audits: Regular security audits are essential for identifying and addressing security vulnerabilities and misconfigurations in domain controller settings. Conduct periodic security assessments, vulnerability scans, and penetration tests to evaluate the effectiveness of hardening measures and identify areas for improvement. Use tools like Microsoft Baseline Security Analyzer (MBSA), PowerShell scripts, and third-party vulnerability scanners to automate the audit process and streamline remediation efforts.

Monitoring and Incident Response: Implement robust monitoring and incident response mechanisms to detect and respond to security incidents in real-time. Configure auditing and logging settings on domain controllers to record security events, authentication attempts, and administrative actions. Use centralized log management solutions, such as Windows Event Forwarding (WEF) or Security Information and Event Management (SIEM) platforms, to aggregate and analyze log data from multiple domain controllers. Establish incident response procedures, including incident triage, investigation, containment, and recovery, to minimize the impact of security breaches and ensure business continuity.

Hardening domain controller configuration settings is a critical aspect of securing Active Directory environments against security threats and vulnerabilities. By implementing a combination of security best practices, such as enforcing strong password policies, disabling unused services, implementing network segmentation, limiting administrative access, and performing regular security audits, organizations can reduce the risk of unauthorized access, data breaches, and service disruptions. Continuous monitoring, incident response, and adaptation to evolving security threats are essential for maintaining the security and resilience of domain controllers and protecting the integrity of Active Directory infrastructure.

Chapter 3: Implementing Role-Based Access Control (RBAC)

Role-Based Access Control (RBAC) is a widely adopted security model that provides a granular and efficient approach to managing access to resources within an organization's Active Directory (AD) environment. RBAC allows administrators to define roles, assign permissions to those roles, and then assign users or groups to those roles based on their responsibilities and job functions. This chapter explores the principles of RBAC and provides guidance on designing RBAC models for Active Directory.

Understanding RBAC Principles: RBAC is based on the principle of least privilege, which states that users should only be granted the minimum permissions required to perform their job functions. RBAC simplifies access management by grouping users into roles and assigning permissions to those roles, rather than managing permissions individually for each user. Key principles of RBAC include:

Role Definition: Identifying and defining roles based on users' job functions, responsibilities, and access requirements within the organization.

Permission Assignment: Assigning permissions to roles based on the tasks and operations associated with each role. Permissions may include read, write, modify, delete, and execute permissions on AD objects and resources.

Role Assignment: Assigning users or groups to roles based on their job roles, responsibilities, and the permissions required to perform their duties effectively.

Separation of Duties (SoD): Ensuring that no single user or role has excessive permissions that could lead to conflicts of interest, misuse of privileges, or security breaches.

Designing RBAC Models: Designing RBAC models for Active Directory involves several key steps, including role identification, permission definition, role assignment, and ongoing management. Here's a structured approach to designing RBAC models:

Identify Roles: Begin by identifying the roles within your organization, such as administrators, managers, help desk personnel, and regular users. Document the responsibilities, tasks, and access requirements associated with each role.

Define Permissions: Define the permissions required for each role based on the tasks and operations performed by users in that role. Use the principle of least privilege to assign only the necessary permissions to each role.

Create Security Groups: Create security groups in Active Directory to represent each role identified in the RBAC model. Use descriptive names for security groups to clearly indicate their purpose and membership criteria.

powershellCopy code

```
New-ADGroup -Name "Administrators" -GroupCategory Security -GroupScope Global -Description "Group for domain administrators"
```

Assign Permissions: Assign the appropriate permissions to each security group based on the permissions defined for the corresponding role. Use tools such as the Active Directory Users and Computers (ADUC) console or PowerShell commands to manage group memberships and permissions.

powershellCopy code

```
Add-ADGroupMember -Identity "Administrators" -Members "JohnDoe", "JaneSmith"
```

Assign Users to Groups: Add users to the security groups corresponding to their roles. Use the ADUC console or

PowerShell commands to manage user memberships and group assignments.

```powershell
powershellCopy code
Add-ADGroupMember -Identity "Administrators" -Members
"JohnDoe", "JaneSmith"
```

Best Practices for RBAC Design: When designing RBAC models for Active Directory, consider the following best practices to ensure effectiveness and efficiency:

Regular Review and Update: Periodically review and update RBAC models to reflect changes in organizational structure, job roles, and access requirements. Remove obsolete roles, update permissions, and adjust role assignments as needed.

Documentation and Documentation: Document RBAC models, including role definitions, permission assignments, and group memberships. Provide clear guidelines and instructions for administrators and users on accessing resources and performing tasks based on their roles.

Testing and Validation: Test RBAC models in a controlled environment to validate their effectiveness and identify any potential issues or conflicts. Conduct user acceptance testing (UAT) to ensure that roles and permissions align with users' expectations and requirements.

Auditing and Monitoring: Implement auditing and monitoring mechanisms to track changes to role assignments, permission modifications, and access requests. Monitor user activity and privilege usage to detect anomalies and potential security incidents.

Designing RBAC models for Active Directory is essential for maintaining security, compliance, and efficiency within an organization's IT infrastructure. By following best practices and principles of RBAC, administrators can streamline access management, reduce the risk of unauthorized access, and improve overall security posture. Regular review, documentation, testing, and monitoring are critical aspects of RBAC design and implementation, ensuring that access controls remain effective and aligned with organizational requirements over time.

Role assignments play a crucial role in Role-Based Access Control (RBAC) systems, including Active Directory (AD), by determining which users or groups are granted specific permissions associated with predefined roles. Configuring and managing role assignments effectively is essential for maintaining security, compliance, and operational efficiency within an organization's IT environment. This chapter explores the process of configuring and managing role assignments in AD, including the use of command-line interface (CLI) commands and best practices for deployment.

Understanding Role Assignments in Active Directory: In Active Directory, role assignments define the relationship between security groups or individual users and the permissions associated with specific roles. Each role assignment grants the members of a security group or individual users access to perform certain tasks or operations within the AD environment. Role assignments are typically managed using Group Policy Objects (GPOs), Access Control Lists (ACLs), or delegated administrative tools.

Configuring Role Assignments Using CLI Commands: Configuring role assignments in Active Directory can be done using various CLI commands, including PowerShell cmdlets and tools such as the Active Directory Users and Computers (ADUC) console. Here are some CLI commands commonly used to configure role assignments:

Adding Users to Security Groups:

```powershell
Copy code
Add-ADGroupMember -Identity "SecurityGroup" -Members "User1", "User2"
```

Adding Users to Organizational Units (OUs):

powershellCopy code

```
Add-ADGroupMember -Identity "OUName" -Members "User1", "User2"
```

Assigning Permissions to Security Groups:

powershellCopy code

```
Add-ADGroupMember -Identity "SecurityGroup" -Members "User1", "User2"
```

Granting Access Rights Using ACLs:

powershellCopy code

```
$ACL = Get-ACL "ADObject" $ACE = New-Object System.DirectoryServices.ActiveDirectoryAccessRule("User1", "ReadProperty", "Allow") $ACL.AddAccessRule($ACE) Set-ACL -Path "ADObject" -AclObject $ACL
```

Best Practices for Managing Role Assignments: Effective management of role assignments requires adherence to best practices to ensure security, compliance, and operational efficiency. Here are some best practices for managing role assignments in Active Directory:

Use Group-Based Assignments: Whenever possible, assign permissions to security groups rather than individual users. Group-based assignments simplify management, allow for easier role-based access control, and facilitate scalability.

Regular Review and Audit: Periodically review and audit role assignments to ensure they align with organizational requirements and adhere to the principle of least privilege. Remove outdated or unnecessary role assignments, and update permissions as needed.

Implement Segregation of Duties (SoD): Implement SoD principles to prevent conflicts of interest and reduce the risk of insider threats. Ensure that no single user or role has excessive permissions that could lead to misuse or abuse of privileges.

Document Role Assignment Policies: Document role assignment policies, including role definitions, permission assignments, and delegation guidelines. Provide clear instructions for administrators and users on accessing resources based on their assigned roles.

Implement Role-Based Access Reviews: Conduct regular access reviews to validate role assignments and ensure that users only have access to the resources required to perform their job functions. Use automated tools or manual processes to streamline access review workflows.

Automating Role Assignment Processes: Automating role assignment processes can streamline operations, improve consistency, and reduce the risk of human error. Consider leveraging PowerShell scripts, Group Policy preferences, or third-party automation tools to automate routine tasks such as adding users to security groups or updating permissions.

Configuring and managing role assignments in Active Directory is a critical aspect of access management and security administration. By following best practices, leveraging CLI commands, and implementing automation where possible, organizations can effectively assign roles, enforce least privilege, and maintain the integrity of their AD environment. Regular review, documentation, and audit of role assignments are essential for ensuring compliance, mitigating risks, and optimizing operational efficiency.

Chapter 4: Hardening Group Policy Settings

Group Policy Objects (GPOs) are powerful tools in Windows environments, allowing administrators to centrally manage and enforce policies across Active Directory domains. However, improper configuration or inadequate security measures can lead to vulnerabilities and potential security breaches. This chapter discusses best practices for securing GPOs to ensure the integrity, confidentiality, and availability of organizational resources.

Limit Access to GPOs: One of the fundamental principles of security is limiting access to sensitive resources. Similarly, access to GPOs should be restricted to authorized personnel only. By default, only members of the Domain Admins group have permissions to create or modify GPOs. To enforce access controls:

Use the Group Policy Management Console (GPMC) or PowerShell to review and adjust permissions on GPOs.

Remove unnecessary users or groups from the GPO permissions list.

Assign permissions based on the principle of least privilege, granting only the necessary permissions to perform specific tasks.

powershellCopy code

```
Get-GPO -All | ForEach-Object {Get-GPO -Name
$_.DisplayName | Set-GPPermission -PermissionLevel
GpoApply -TargetName "GroupOrUser" -TargetType
Group/User}
```

Secure GPOs with Strong Passwords: GPOs can contain sensitive configuration settings, and compromising them could have serious consequences. It's essential to protect GPOs with strong passwords to prevent unauthorized modifications. Set strong passwords for GPOs and regularly rotate them according to your organization's password policy.

Use the Group Policy Management Console (GPMC) to modify the password settings for GPOs.

Ensure that passwords meet complexity requirements and are not easily guessable.

powershellCopy code

```
Set-GPO -Name "GPOName" -Password ("NewPassword" |
ConvertTo-SecureString -AsPlainText -Force)
```

Implement GPO Filtering: GPOs apply to users and computers within their scope, but sometimes it's necessary to apply policies selectively based on specific criteria. GPO filtering allows administrators to target policies to specific users, groups, or computers. Use security filtering and WMI filtering to ensure that GPOs apply only where intended.

Use the GPMC to configure security filtering for GPOs, specifying the users or groups to which the GPO applies.

Create WMI filters to further refine GPO targeting based on computer attributes.

powershellCopy code

```
Set-GPPermission -Name "GPOName" -TargetName
"GroupOrUser" -TargetType Group/User -PermissionLevel
GpoApply
```

Monitor and Audit GPO Changes: Keeping track of changes to GPOs is crucial for maintaining security and compliance. Implement auditing mechanisms to monitor modifications to GPOs and detect unauthorized changes promptly. Regularly review audit logs to identify potential security incidents or policy violations.

Enable GPO auditing through Group Policy settings or Advanced Audit Policy Configuration.

Configure audit policies to monitor changes to GPOs and related objects in Active Directory.

powershellCopy code

```
Set-GPRegistryValue    -Name    "GPOName"    -Key "RegistryKeyPath" -ValueName "ValueName" -Type DWord -Value 1
```

Regularly Back Up GPOs: GPOs represent critical configurations that can significantly impact the operation of your IT infrastructure. Regularly backing up GPOs ensures that you can recover from accidental deletions, corruption, or other issues quickly.

Use the GPMC or PowerShell to back up GPOs regularly.

Store GPO backups in a secure location, separate from the production environment.

powershellCopy code

```
Backup-GPO -All -Path "BackupPath"
```

Test GPO Changes in a Lab Environment: Before deploying GPO changes in a production environment, it's advisable to test them thoroughly in a lab or test environment. Testing helps identify potential issues or conflicts before they impact users or systems.

Use a separate test domain or isolated environment to simulate GPO changes.

Test GPO modifications on representative user and computer configurations to ensure compatibility and effectiveness.

powershellCopy code

```
Invoke-GPUpdate -Computer "ComputerName" -Force
```

Regularly Review GPO Settings: Over time, business requirements, security standards, and technology landscapes may change, necessitating adjustments to GPO settings. Regularly review GPO configurations to ensure they remain aligned with organizational goals and security best practices.

Conduct periodic reviews of GPO settings, including policies, preferences, and administrative templates.

Update GPOs as needed to reflect changes in security requirements, compliance regulations, or business processes.

powershellCopy code

```
Get-GPOReport -Name "GPOName" -ReportType HTML -
Path "ReportPath.html"
```

In summary, securing Group Policy Objects (GPOs) is critical for maintaining the security and integrity of an organization's Active Directory environment. By implementing the best practices outlined Next, administrators can mitigate security risks, enforce compliance, and ensure the effective management of GPOs across the enterprise.

Group Policy is a powerful tool for managing and configuring settings in Windows environments. However, with great power comes great responsibility, and ensuring the security of Group Policy Objects (GPOs) is paramount. This chapter delves into advanced techniques for hardening Group Policy to enhance security posture and mitigate potential vulnerabilities.

Utilizing Advanced Security Filtering: Security filtering allows administrators to control which users or groups apply a particular GPO. Advanced security filtering techniques enable granular control over GPO application based on various attributes, including user properties, computer characteristics, or organizational units.

WMI Filtering: Windows Management Instrumentation (WMI) filtering allows administrators to apply GPOs based on specific conditions, such as hardware configurations or software installations.

```powershell
Get-WmiObject -Class Win32_OperatingSystem | Where-Object {$_.Version -eq "10.0.18363"}
```

LDAP Filtering: Lightweight Directory Access Protocol (LDAP) filtering enables targeting GPOs based on custom LDAP queries, offering flexibility in defining the scope of GPO application.

```powershell
(&(objectCategory=user)(memberOf=CN=Admins,CN=Users,
DC=domain,DC=com))
```

Implementing GPO Version Control: Version control for GPOs ensures accountability, facilitates rollback in case of misconfigurations, and supports change management processes. Advanced techniques involve leveraging version control systems or dedicated GPO management solutions to track changes, compare versions, and enforce approval workflows.

Group Policy Management Console (GPMC): GPMC provides built-in capabilities for viewing GPO version history and comparing revisions. Regularly export GPO backups and maintain a repository for historical tracking.

```powershell
Get-GPO -Name "GPOName" | Get-GPOReport -ReportType
XML -Path "C:\GPOBackups\GPOName_backup.xml"
```

Third-party GPO Management Tools: Commercial solutions like Specops, Netwrix, or ManageEngine offer advanced features for GPO versioning, change tracking, and compliance reporting.

Enforcing GPO Signing and Verification: GPO signing enhances security by ensuring the integrity and authenticity of GPOs. Enabling GPO signing requires the use of a certificate issued by a trusted certification authority (CA) and configuring clients to verify GPO signatures during processing.

Enabling GPO Signing: Use the Group Policy Management Console (GPMC) to enable GPO signing in the Default Domain Policy or specific GPOs.

powershellCopy code

```
Set-GPRegistryValue -Name "GPOName" -Key "HKLM\SOFTWARE\Microsoft\Windows NT\CurrentVersion\Winlogon" -ValueName "SecureServerAuthority" -Type DWord -Value 1
```

Configuring Client Verification: Ensure that client machines have the "Always wait for the network at computer startup and logon" policy enabled to allow time for GPO signature verification during startup.

powershellCopy code

```
Set-GPRegistryValue -Name "GPOName" -Key "HKLM\SOFTWARE\Policies\Microsoft\Windows NT\CurrentVersion\Winlogon" -ValueName "SyncForegroundPolicy" -Type DWord -Value 1
```

Implementing GPO Delegation and Role-Based Access Control (RBAC): Delegating GPO management tasks to specific administrators or groups helps distribute responsibilities and reduce the risk of inadvertent misconfigurations. RBAC ensures that only authorized personnel have access to modify or deploy GPOs.

Delegate GPO Management: Use the Delegation tab in the GPMC to assign permissions to specific users or groups for managing GPOs.

powershellCopy code

```
Set-GPPermission -Name "GPOName" -PermissionLevel GpoEdit -TargetName "UserOrGroup" -TargetType User/Group
```

Implement RBAC Policies: Define RBAC policies to govern access to GPMC and restrict privileges based on administrative roles.

powershellCopy code

```
New-ADGroup -Name "GPOAdministrators" -GroupCategory Security -GroupScope Global
```

Monitoring GPO Activity and Auditing: Comprehensive monitoring and auditing of GPO activity are essential for detecting unauthorized changes, troubleshooting issues, and maintaining compliance with security policies.

Enable GPO Auditing: Configure advanced audit policies to track changes to GPOs and related objects in Active Directory.

powershellCopy code

```
Set-GPRegistryValue -Name "GPOName" -Key "HKLM\SOFTWARE\Policies\Microsoft\Windows NT\CurrentVersion\Winlogon" -ValueName "AuditGPOs" -Type DWord -Value 1
```

Review Audit Logs: Regularly review security event logs on domain controllers to identify suspicious activities or unauthorized modifications to GPOs.

In summary, implementing advanced techniques for Group Policy hardening is crucial for enhancing the security posture of Windows environments. By leveraging advanced security filtering, version control, GPO signing, delegation, and auditing mechanisms, organizations can strengthen GPO security, mitigate risks, and maintain compliance with regulatory requirements.

Chapter 5: Active Directory Auditing and Monitoring

Auditing is a critical component of any organization's security strategy, providing visibility into activities occurring within the Active Directory environment. By configuring auditing policies, administrators can track user actions, monitor changes to sensitive data, and detect potential security incidents. This chapter explores the process of configuring auditing policies for Active Directory, including the necessary steps and CLI commands.

Understanding Auditing in Active Directory: Auditing in Active Directory involves monitoring and recording events related to directory objects, authentication attempts, access control modifications, and administrative activities. By enabling auditing, organizations can maintain compliance, investigate security breaches, and ensure accountability.

Enabling Auditing at the Domain Level: Auditing settings can be configured at the domain level to apply to all objects within the domain. To enable auditing for Active Directory objects, administrators can use Group Policy or PowerShell commands.

Using Group Policy:

Open the Group Policy Management Console (GPMC).

Navigate to the Group Policy Object (GPO) linked to the domain.

Edit the GPO and navigate to Computer Configuration -> Policies -> Windows Settings -> Security Settings -> Advanced Audit Policy Configuration.

Configure audit policies based on specific requirements, such as auditing object access, account management, or directory service access.

powershellCopy code

```
Set-ItemProperty                        -Path
"HKLM:\System\CurrentControlSet\Services\NTDS\Param
eters" -Name "AuditLevel" -Value 3
```

Configuring Auditing for Specific Active Directory Objects: Administrators may want to enable auditing for specific Active Directory objects, such as user accounts, groups, or organizational units (OUs). This allows for more granular monitoring and tracking of changes to critical resources.

Using PowerShell:

Identify the object for which auditing needs to be enabled. Use the Set-ADObject cmdlet to configure auditing settings for the specified object.

powershellCopy code

```
Set-ADObject                            -Identity
"CN=User1,OU=Users,DC=contoso,DC=com"        -Add
@{"Add"="Everyone"; "Delete"="Everyone"}
```

Defining Auditing Scope and Granularity: When configuring auditing policies, it's essential to define the scope and granularity of auditing based on organizational requirements and security objectives. This includes determining which events to audit, specifying audit settings, and establishing thresholds for event log retention.

Using Group Policy:

Define audit policies for specific categories of events, such as account logon events, account management, directory service access, or object access.

Specify audit settings, including success or failure auditing, to track desired activities.

Configure advanced audit policy settings to enhance granularity and reduce noise in audit logs.

powershellCopy code

```
Auditpol /set /subcategory:"Directory Service Changes" /success:enable /failure:enable
```

Monitoring and Reviewing Audit Logs: Once auditing policies are configured, it's crucial to monitor and review audit logs regularly. This involves analyzing event logs, correlating audit data, and responding to security incidents or policy violations.

Using Event Viewer:

Open the Event Viewer console on a domain controller or administrative workstation.

Navigate to the Security log to view audit events related to Active Directory.

Filter audit logs based on event IDs, usernames, event types, or specific activities of interest.

powershellCopy code

```
Get-EventLog -LogName Security -InstanceId 4662 | Select-Object -Property TimeGenerated, EventID, Message
```

Responding to Security Incidents: In the event of a security incident or policy violation, administrators must take appropriate action to investigate, contain, and remediate the issue. This may involve identifying compromised accounts, restoring deleted objects, or implementing additional security measures.

Using PowerShell:

Analyze audit logs to identify suspicious activities or unauthorized changes.

Disable compromised user accounts or reset passwords to prevent further unauthorized access.

Restore deleted objects from Active Directory Recycle Bin or backups if necessary.

powershellCopy code

Search-ADAccount -AccountDisabled | Disable-ADAccount

In summary, configuring auditing policies for Active Directory is essential for maintaining security, compliance, and accountability within an organization. By enabling auditing, defining the scope and granularity of audit settings, monitoring audit logs, and responding to security incidents, administrators can effectively safeguard Active Directory environments against potential threats and vulnerabilities.

Active Directory (AD) serves as the cornerstone of many organizations' IT infrastructure, managing user accounts, groups, permissions, and other critical resources. Ensuring the security and integrity of Active Directory is paramount, and one of the key components of maintaining a secure environment is monitoring and analyzing audit logs. Next, we will explore the importance of monitoring Active Directory audit logs, techniques for analyzing log data, and the use of command-line interface (CLI) commands to facilitate these processes.

Understanding the Importance of Audit Logs: Audit logs provide a detailed record of events occurring within Active Directory, including user logon attempts, changes to group memberships, modifications to directory objects, and administrative activities. By monitoring audit logs, organizations can detect suspicious behavior, track changes, and investigate security incidents.

Enabling Audit Policies in Active Directory: Before monitoring audit logs, administrators must ensure that appropriate audit policies are enabled in Active Directory. This involves configuring audit settings to capture relevant events and activities.

Using Group Policy:

Open the Group Policy Management Console (GPMC).

Navigate to the appropriate Group Policy Object (GPO) linked to the domain or organizational unit.

Configure audit policies under Computer Configuration -> Policies -> Windows Settings -> Security Settings -> Advanced Audit Policy Configuration.

powershellCopy code

```
auditpol /set /subcategory:"Directory Service Changes" /success:enable /failure:enable
```

Monitoring Audit Logs in Real-Time: Real-time monitoring allows administrators to detect and respond to security incidents as they occur. Various tools and utilities can be used to monitor Active Directory audit logs in real-time.

Using PowerShell: PowerShell provides cmdlets to retrieve and filter events from the Windows event logs, including the Security log where Active Directory audit events are recorded.

powershellCopy code

```
Get-WinEvent -LogName Security -MaxEvents 100 | Where-Object { $_.ID -eq 4740 }
```

Analyzing Audit Logs for Security Incidents: Analyzing audit logs involves examining log data to identify patterns, anomalies, and indicators of compromise. This process helps organizations detect unauthorized access, data breaches, and other security threats.

Identifying Failed Logon Attempts: Failed logon attempts may indicate brute-force attacks or unauthorized access attempts. Analyzing event logs for failed logon events can help identify potential security incidents.

powershellCopy code

```
Get-WinEvent -LogName Security -FilterHashtable
@{LogName='Security'; ID=4625}
```

Detecting Changes to Group Memberships: Changes to group memberships can impact access control and privilege escalation. Monitoring audit logs for group membership modifications can help organizations identify unauthorized changes.

powershellCopy code

```
Get-WinEvent -LogName Security -FilterXPath
"*[System[EventID=4732 or EventID=4733]]"
```

Automating Log Analysis with SIEM Solutions: Security Information and Event Management (SIEM) solutions offer advanced capabilities for aggregating, correlating, and analyzing log data from multiple sources, including Active Directory.

Deploying SIEM Solutions: Deploying a SIEM solution involves installing and configuring the software, integrating it with Active Directory and other data sources, and defining correlation rules and alerts.

Using SIEM Dashboards: SIEM dashboards provide centralized visibility into security events and trends, allowing administrators to quickly identify and respond to potential threats.

Implementing Log Retention Policies: Log retention policies dictate how long audit logs should be retained for compliance, forensic analysis, and troubleshooting purposes. Organizations should establish and enforce log retention policies to ensure that audit data is retained for the required duration.

Configuring Log Retention Settings: Log retention settings can be configured in Active Directory or SIEM solutions to specify the retention period and storage location for audit logs.

powershellCopy code

```
auditpol /set /retention:365
```

In summary, monitoring and analyzing Active Directory audit logs are essential components of an effective cybersecurity strategy. By enabling audit policies, monitoring logs in real-time, analyzing log data for security incidents, and leveraging SIEM solutions, organizations can enhance their ability to detect, respond to, and mitigate security threats in Active Directory environments.

Chapter 6: Implementing Multi-Factor Authentication (MFA)

In today's digital landscape, securing user access to sensitive data and resources is paramount for organizations of all sizes. Traditional authentication methods, such as passwords, have proven susceptible to various cyber threats, including phishing, brute-force attacks, and credential stuffing. As a result, there has been a growing emphasis on implementing Multi-Factor Authentication (MFA) solutions to augment traditional password-based authentication and enhance security posture. This chapter delves into the fundamentals of MFA solutions and explores various authentication methods employed to verify user identities.

Introduction to Multi-Factor Authentication (MFA): Multi-Factor Authentication (MFA) is a security mechanism that requires users to provide two or more forms of verification before gaining access to a system or application. By combining multiple factors, such as something the user knows (password), something the user has (security token), or something the user is (biometric data), MFA significantly strengthens authentication and mitigates the risk of unauthorized access.

Authentication Factors: MFA solutions typically leverage three primary authentication factors:

Something You Know: This factor involves knowledge-based authentication, such as passwords, PINs, or security questions. While passwords remain a common authentication method, they are prone to vulnerabilities, such as password reuse and brute-force attacks.

Something You Have: This factor relies on possession-based authentication, such as smart cards, security tokens, or mobile devices. Users must physically possess the token or device to authenticate successfully.

Something You Are: Also known as biometric authentication, this factor verifies the user's identity based on unique physiological or behavioral characteristics, such as fingerprints, facial recognition, or voice recognition.

Types of MFA Solutions: MFA solutions come in various forms, each offering different levels of security and user experience. Some common types of MFA solutions include:

One-Time Password (OTP) Tokens: OTP tokens generate temporary codes that users must enter along with their passwords during the authentication process. These tokens can be hardware-based (e.g., RSA SecurID tokens) or software-based (e.g., Google Authenticator).

Push Notifications: Mobile-based MFA solutions send push notifications to users' smartphones, prompting them to approve or deny login attempts. Users can authenticate with a single tap on their mobile devices.

Biometric Authentication: Biometric MFA solutions use unique physical or behavioral characteristics to verify users' identities. Common biometric modalities include fingerprints, facial recognition, iris scans, and voice recognition.

Smart Cards: Smart card-based MFA solutions require users to insert a physical smart card into a card reader and enter a PIN to authenticate. Smart cards store digital certificates and cryptographic keys for secure authentication.

Deploying MFA Solutions: Deploying an MFA solution involves several steps, including:

Assessment and Planning: Assess the organization's authentication requirements, evaluate available MFA solutions, and develop a deployment plan tailored to the organization's needs.

Integration with Identity Providers: Integrate the chosen MFA solution with existing identity providers, such as Active Directory, LDAP, or cloud-based identity platforms, to enable seamless authentication workflows.

User Enrollment: Onboard users onto the MFA platform, educate them about the authentication process, and guide them through the enrollment process for registering authentication factors.

Configuration and Policy Management: Configure MFA policies, such as authentication methods, enforcement rules, and access controls, to align with security policies and regulatory requirements.

Monitoring and Maintenance: Continuously monitor MFA usage, analyze authentication logs for suspicious activities, and perform regular maintenance tasks, such as software updates and policy adjustments.

Challenges and Considerations: While MFA offers significant security benefits, organizations must address certain challenges and considerations when implementing MFA solutions:

User Experience: Balancing security with user experience is crucial to ensure seamless authentication workflows and minimize user friction.

Integration Complexity: Integrating MFA solutions with existing IT infrastructure and applications may pose challenges, requiring careful planning and coordination.

Cost and Scalability: MFA solutions vary in cost and scalability, and organizations must consider factors such as licensing fees, hardware requirements, and scalability options.

Regulatory Compliance: Compliance with industry regulations and data protection laws may dictate specific MFA requirements, such as strong authentication for accessing sensitive data or financial transactions.

In summary, Multi-Factor Authentication (MFA) solutions play a vital role in enhancing security by requiring users to provide multiple forms of verification during the authentication process. By understanding the principles of MFA, deploying appropriate authentication methods, and addressing deployment challenges, organizations can bolster their defenses against evolving cyber threats and safeguard sensitive data and resources.

Multi-Factor Authentication (MFA) has become a critical component of modern cybersecurity strategies, offering an additional layer of protection beyond traditional password-based authentication. In the context of Active Directory (AD), deploying and managing MFA entails integrating MFA solutions with AD infrastructure, enrolling users, configuring authentication policies, and monitoring MFA usage. This chapter explores the process of deploying and managing MFA for Active Directory, encompassing the necessary steps, best practices, and CLI commands involved.

Understanding the Need for MFA in Active Directory: Active Directory serves as the cornerstone of identity and access management in many organizations, containing user accounts, groups, and access permissions. However, relying solely on passwords for authentication poses inherent security risks, as passwords can be compromised through various means. MFA mitigates these risks by requiring additional forms of authentication, such as biometrics or one-time passcodes, thereby enhancing security.

Choosing an MFA Solution for Active Directory: Before deploying MFA in an Active Directory environment, organizations must evaluate different MFA solutions to find the one that best fits their requirements. Factors to consider include compatibility with AD infrastructure, support for various authentication methods, ease of integration, scalability, and regulatory compliance.

Integration with Active Directory: Integrating an MFA solution with Active Directory involves configuring AD to authenticate users using the MFA system. This typically requires installing and configuring additional software components or agents on domain controllers or authentication servers.

Installing MFA Agents: Use CLI commands to install MFA agents on domain controllers or dedicated authentication servers.

bashCopy code

```
msiexec /i MFA-Agent.msi /quiet /qn /norestart
```

Configuring Integration Settings: Configure integration settings to establish communication between AD and the MFA system. This may involve specifying the IP address or hostname of the MFA server and configuring authentication protocols.

User Enrollment and Registration: After integrating MFA with Active Directory, users need to enroll in the MFA system and register their authentication factors. This process varies depending on the chosen MFA solution but typically involves accessing a self-service portal or using CLI commands to initiate enrollment.

User Enrollment Portal: Provide users with access to a self-service enrollment portal where they can register authentication factors, such as mobile devices or security tokens.

arduinoCopy code

https://mfa-enrollment.example.com

CLI Enrollment Commands: Alternatively, administrators can use CLI commands to initiate enrollment for users or groups.

cssCopy code

```
mfa enroll --username user1
```

Configuring MFA Policies: Once users are enrolled in the MFA system, administrators can configure MFA policies to specify when and how MFA should be enforced. This includes defining authentication requirements based on user roles, groups, or network locations.

CLI Configuration Commands: Use CLI commands to configure MFA policies, such as requiring MFA for specific user groups or setting session timeouts.

csharpCopy code

```
mfa policy set --group "Finance" --require-mfa --session-timeout 30
```

Monitoring MFA Usage and Performance: Continuous monitoring of MFA usage and performance is essential to ensure the effectiveness of the MFA deployment and identify any anomalies or issues. Administrators can use CLI commands to retrieve MFA usage statistics, view authentication logs, and troubleshoot authentication failures.

CLI Monitoring Commands: Use CLI commands to query MFA logs, retrieve authentication statistics, and monitor system performance.

cssCopy code

mfa logs --user user1

Maintenance and Updates: Regular maintenance and updates are necessary to keep the MFA system secure and up-to-date with the latest features and security patches. Administrators should establish a schedule for performing routine maintenance tasks, such as software updates, database backups, and system checks.

CLI Update Commands: Use CLI commands to download and install updates for the MFA software components.

sqlCopy code

mfa update --component agent

In summary, deploying and managing MFA for Active Directory requires careful planning, integration, and configuration to ensure a seamless and secure authentication experience for users. By following best practices, leveraging CLI commands for deployment and management tasks, and regularly monitoring MFA usage and performance, organizations can strengthen their security posture and mitigate the risk of unauthorized access to AD resources.

Chapter 7: Securing Privileged Accounts and Service Accounts

In the realm of cybersecurity, the principle of least privilege (PoLP) stands as a cornerstone for ensuring the security and integrity of systems and data. The concept revolves around restricting user access rights and permissions to the minimum levels required to perform their duties effectively. By adhering to the principle of least privilege, organizations can minimize the risk of unauthorized access, limit the potential damage caused by insider threats, and enhance overall security posture. This chapter delves into the importance of implementing least privilege principles, strategies for its implementation, and the utilization of CLI commands to enforce least privilege policies within an organization's IT infrastructure.

Understanding the Principle of Least Privilege: At its core, the principle of least privilege advocates granting users only the permissions necessary to carry out their specific tasks or roles within an organization. This approach contrasts with the traditional model of granting excessive permissions based on user roles or hierarchical positions, which often results in unnecessary access to sensitive resources and increases the attack surface.

Benefits of Implementing Least Privilege: Implementing least privilege principles yields several significant benefits:

Reduced Attack Surface: By limiting user privileges to the bare minimum required for their roles, organizations can minimize the potential entry points for attackers and reduce the likelihood of successful exploitation of vulnerabilities.

Mitigated Insider Threats: Restricting user access helps mitigate the risk of insider threats, as employees or malicious insiders cannot abuse excessive privileges to compromise sensitive data or systems.

Enhanced Compliance: Adhering to least privilege principles aids in achieving regulatory compliance requirements, such as GDPR, HIPAA, or PCI DSS, by ensuring that access to sensitive data is strictly controlled and monitored.

Improved Security Posture: Overall, implementing least privilege enhances an organization's security posture by fostering a proactive approach to access control and minimizing the impact of security incidents.

Strategies for Implementing Least Privilege: Implementing least privilege principles involves several key strategies:

Role-Based Access Control (RBAC): RBAC assigns permissions to users based on their roles or job functions, ensuring that each user has precisely the privileges necessary to fulfill their responsibilities. CLI commands play a crucial role in configuring RBAC policies within an organization's systems and applications.

cssCopy code

rbac configure --role "Finance Manager" --permissions "Read-Only Access to Financial Data"

Privilege Escalation Controls: Organizations should implement controls to manage privilege escalation, ensuring that users cannot elevate their privileges without proper authorization. This may involve configuring User Account Control (UAC) settings on Windows systems or implementing sudo policies on Unix/Linux systems.

scssCopy code

uac configure --level "Medium" --prompt "Always Notify"

Continuous Monitoring and Auditing: Regularly monitoring user access and auditing privileges are essential components of least privilege implementation. CLI commands can be used to retrieve audit logs, review access permissions, and detect any deviations from least privilege policies.

bashCopy code

```
audit log view --user "JohnDoe" --date "2024-02-16"
```

Automated Privilege Management: Leveraging automation tools and scripts can streamline the process of enforcing least privilege policies across an organization's IT infrastructure. CLI commands can be incorporated into automation scripts to automate tasks such as user provisioning, access reviews, and privilege revocation.

Copy code

```
script automate_privilege_management.sh
```

Challenges and Considerations: While implementing least privilege principles offers numerous benefits, organizations may encounter certain challenges:

Balancing Security and Productivity: Striking the right balance between security and productivity is crucial, as overly restrictive access controls may impede user workflows and hinder productivity.

User Education and Awareness: Educating users about the importance of least privilege and the rationale behind access restrictions is essential for fostering a security-conscious culture within the organization.

Legacy Systems and Applications: Legacy systems and applications may not support granular access controls or RBAC, making it challenging to enforce least privilege principles uniformly across all IT assets.

Ongoing Maintenance and Review: Regularly reviewing and updating access permissions, roles, and policies is necessary to adapt to changing business requirements and mitigate the risk of privilege creep.

In summary, implementing least privilege principles is paramount for organizations seeking to bolster their cybersecurity defenses and mitigate the risk of unauthorized access and insider threats. By adopting strategies such as role-based access control, privilege escalation controls, continuous monitoring, and automation, organizations can enforce least privilege policies effectively across their IT environments. Leveraging CLI commands to configure access controls, audit privileges, and automate privilege management tasks facilitates the implementation and maintenance of least privilege principles within an organization's cybersecurity framework.

Service accounts play a pivotal role in the functionality and security of modern IT environments. These accounts are designed to provide applications, services, and processes with the necessary permissions to perform specific tasks or access resources within an organization's network. However, managing and securing service accounts present unique challenges and considerations, as they often possess elevated privileges and can become prime targets for attackers if not properly configured. This chapter explores the importance of managing and securing service accounts, strategies for their effective management, and the utilization of CLI commands to implement security measures within an organization's infrastructure.

Understanding Service Accounts: Service accounts are non-human accounts used by services, applications, and processes to interact with various components of an IT environment. Unlike user accounts, service accounts typically do not correspond to individual users and are dedicated solely to performing automated tasks or providing access to resources.

The Importance of Service Account Management: Effective management of service accounts is essential for maintaining the security and integrity of an organization's IT infrastructure. Poorly managed service accounts can pose significant security risks, including unauthorized access, privilege escalation, and potential system compromise. Therefore, organizations must implement robust practices for managing and securing service accounts.

Strategies for Managing Service Accounts: Managing service accounts involves several key strategies aimed at ensuring their proper configuration, monitoring, and control:

Inventory and Documentation: Begin by conducting an inventory of all service accounts in use within the organization. Document the purpose, owner, and associated permissions for each service account to maintain visibility and accountability.

Least Privilege Principle: Apply the principle of least privilege to service accounts by granting them only the permissions necessary to perform their intended tasks. Use CLI commands to review and adjust permissions as needed.

arduinoCopy code

```
account set-permissions --account service_account --permissions read-only
```

Regular Password Rotation: Implement a policy for regularly rotating service account passwords to reduce the risk of credential theft and unauthorized access. CLI commands can automate password rotation tasks, ensuring compliance with security policies.

cssCopy code

```
account rotate-password --account service_account --interval monthly
```

Monitoring and Logging: Implement monitoring and logging mechanisms to track the activities of service accounts and detect any suspicious or unauthorized behavior. CLI commands can retrieve logs and generate reports for analysis.

cssCopy code

```
log view --account service_account --date-range "2024-
01-01 to 2024-02-01"
```

Segregation of Duties: Avoid using service accounts with excessive privileges or broad access rights. Instead, segregate duties and responsibilities to limit the potential impact of compromised service accounts.

Securing Service Account Credentials: Service account credentials must be adequately protected to prevent unauthorized access and misuse. Consider the following security measures:

Credential Encryption: Store service account passwords and credentials in encrypted form to prevent unauthorized disclosure. Utilize encryption tools and techniques to safeguard sensitive information.

Credential Vaults: Implement secure credential vaults or password management solutions to centralize and manage service account credentials securely. CLI commands can interact with these vaults to retrieve and update credentials as needed.

sqlCopy code

```
vault get-credentials --account service_account
```

Credential Rotation Policies: Enforce policies for regularly rotating service account credentials to mitigate the risk of credential theft and unauthorized access. CLI commands can automate the credential rotation process according to predefined schedules.

cssCopy code

```
vault rotate-credentials --account service_account --
interval quarterly
```

Best Practices for Service Account Security: Adopting best practices can further enhance the security of service accounts:

Regular Audits: Conduct periodic audits of service accounts to identify inactive or obsolete accounts that can be safely decommissioned.

Secure Configuration Management: Implement secure configuration management practices for service accounts, including disabling unnecessary protocols, limiting remote access, and enforcing strong authentication methods.

Access Control: Ensure that service accounts have access only to the resources required for their designated tasks. Use CLI commands to review and adjust access permissions as necessary.

arduinoCopy code

```
account set-access --account service_account --resources "/path/to/resource" --permissions read-write
```

Incident Response: Develop incident response procedures to address security incidents involving service accounts promptly. CLI commands can facilitate incident investigation and response activities by retrieving relevant logs and audit trails.

cssCopy code

```
incident-response analyze --account service_account --incident-type unauthorized-access
```

In summary, managing and securing service accounts is a critical aspect of maintaining the overall security posture of an organization's IT infrastructure. By implementing robust management practices, adhering to security principles such as least privilege, and leveraging CLI commands for configuration, monitoring, and automation, organizations can effectively mitigate the risks associated with service accounts and safeguard their sensitive data and resources from unauthorized access and misuse.

Chapter 8: Active Directory Federation Services (AD FS) Security

Active Directory Federation Services (AD FS) is a crucial component in modern identity and access management (IAM) architectures, facilitating single sign-on (SSO) authentication across disparate systems and applications. However, the security of AD FS endpoints and token issuance mechanisms is paramount to prevent unauthorized access, protect sensitive data, and maintain compliance with regulatory requirements. This chapter explores various techniques and best practices for securing AD FS endpoints and token issuance, along with practical CLI commands to deploy these security measures effectively.

Understanding AD FS Endpoints: AD FS endpoints serve as entry points for authentication requests and token issuance within the federation environment. These endpoints include the federation metadata endpoint, the authentication endpoint, the token issuance endpoint, and the WS-Federation passive authentication endpoint. Securing these endpoints is crucial to prevent unauthorized access and potential security breaches.

Importance of Securing AD FS Endpoints: Securing AD FS endpoints is essential for maintaining the confidentiality, integrity, and availability of authentication services and user data. Failure to adequately secure endpoints can expose sensitive information, compromise user identities, and undermine the trustworthiness of the federation infrastructure.

Techniques for Securing AD FS Endpoints: Securing AD FS endpoints involves implementing various security measures and best practices:

Transport Layer Security (TLS) Encryption: Encrypting communication between clients and AD FS endpoints using TLS is essential to prevent eavesdropping and man-in-the-middle attacks. Use CLI commands to configure TLS settings and certificate management.

cssCopy code

```
tls configure --endpoint adfs --protocol tls1.2 --certificate <certificate_name>
```

Endpoint Hardening: Implement security controls such as IP whitelisting, rate limiting, and request validation to protect AD FS endpoints from unauthorized access and denial-of-service (DoS) attacks.

scssCopy code

```
endpoint configure --name authentication --whitelist <IP_range> --rate-limit 100 --request-validation strict
```

Multi-Factor Authentication (MFA): Enforce MFA for authentication requests to AD FS endpoints to enhance security and mitigate the risk of unauthorized access. CLI commands can configure MFA settings and enforce MFA policies.

cssCopy code

```
mfa configure --endpoint authentication --method sms --method totp --enforce-policy true
```

Token Issuance Policies: Define and enforce token issuance policies to ensure that only authorized users and applications receive access tokens. Use CLI commands to configure token issuance rules and access control policies.

cssCopy code

```
token-policy configure --endpoint token-issuance --issuer <issuer_name> --audience <audience_name> --validity-period 3600
```

Audit Logging and Monitoring: Enable audit logging and monitoring for AD FS endpoints to detect and investigate security incidents promptly. CLI commands can retrieve and analyze audit logs for suspicious activities.

cCopy code

```
audit-log enable --endpoint adfs --log-level detailed
```

Best Practices for Token Issuance Security: Implementing best practices for token issuance security enhances the overall security posture of AD FS:

Token Signing and Encryption: Sign and encrypt issued tokens using strong cryptographic algorithms to prevent tampering and unauthorized access.

cssCopy code

```
token-policy configure --endpoint token-issuance --signing-algorithm RS256 --encryption-algorithm A256GCM
```

Token Revocation: Implement token revocation mechanisms to invalidate issued tokens in case of compromised credentials or security breaches.

cssCopy code

```
token-revocation configure --endpoint token-issuance --revocation-list <revocation_list_name> --automatic-revocation true
```

Token Scope Limitations: Limit the scope and permissions granted by issued tokens to minimize the risk of privilege escalation and unauthorized access.

cssCopy code

```
token-policy configure --endpoint token-issuance --scope-limitations read-only --scope-duration 3600
```

Continuous Improvement and Risk Mitigation: Regularly assess and update security measures for AD FS endpoints to address emerging threats and vulnerabilities. Conduct security assessments, penetration testing, and vulnerability scans to identify and remediate security weaknesses proactively.

In summary, securing AD FS endpoints and token issuance mechanisms is critical for safeguarding authentication services and protecting sensitive data within federation environments. By implementing robust security measures, enforcing access controls, and monitoring endpoint activities, organizations can mitigate the risk of unauthorized access, data breaches, and compliance violations. Leveraging CLI commands enables administrators to configure and manage security settings effectively, ensuring the integrity and reliability of AD FS deployments.

Trust relationships and claims authorization rules are fundamental components of Active Directory Federation Services (AD FS) deployments, enabling secure authentication and access control in federated identity environments. Establishing trust relationships between identity providers (IdPs) and relying parties (RPs) allows users to authenticate seamlessly across different domains or organizations. Additionally, claims authorization rules define access control policies based on user attributes or claims, determining which resources users can access. This chapter explores the configuration of trust relationships and claims authorization rules in AD FS, including practical CLI commands for deployment and management.

Understanding Trust Relationships: Trust relationships in AD FS define the level of trust and authentication mechanisms between different entities within a federation environment. These entities may include IdPs, RPs, or federated partners. Establishing trust relationships allows for secure authentication and communication between these entities, enabling seamless access to resources across organizational boundaries.

Types of Trust Relationships: AD FS supports several types of trust relationships, including:

Federation Trust: A federation trust is established between the AD FS server and external IdPs or federation partners. This trust allows users to authenticate with their home organization's identity provider and access resources in the relying party's domain.

Claims Provider Trust: A claims provider trust is established between the AD FS server and external claims providers, such as Active Directory or LDAP directories. This trust allows the AD FS server to accept claims from the external provider and use them for authentication and authorization purposes.

Relying Party Trust: A relying party trust is established between the AD FS server and external RPs or applications. This trust allows the RP to trust the AD FS server for authentication and authorization, enabling single sign-on (SSO) and access control based on claims.

Configuring Trust Relationships: Configuring trust relationships in AD FS involves the following steps:

Create Federation Trust: Use the **Add-AdfsClaimsProviderTrust** CLI command to add a new federation trust with an external IdP or federation partner.

sqlCopy code

```
Add-AdfsClaimsProviderTrust -Name "External IdP" -MetadataUrl "https://externalidp.com/metadata.xml"
```

Create Claims Provider Trust: Use the **Add-AdfsClaimsProviderTrust** CLI command to add a new claims provider trust with an external claims provider.

sqlCopy code

```
Add-AdfsClaimsProviderTrust -Name "External Claims Provider" -MetadataUrl "https://externalcp.com/metadata.xml"
```

Create Relying Party Trust: Use the **Add-AdfsRelyingPartyTrust** CLI command to add a new relying party trust with an external RP or application.

sqlCopy code

Add-AdfsRelyingPartyTrust -Name "External Relying Party" - MetadataUrl "https://externalrp.com/metadata.xml"

Understanding Claims Authorization Rules: Claims authorization rules in AD FS define the conditions under which users are granted access to resources based on their claims or attributes. These rules evaluate incoming claims and determine whether to allow or deny access to specific resources or applications.

Types of Claims Authorization Rules: AD FS supports various types of claims authorization rules, including:

Permit Rules: Permit rules allow access to resources if certain conditions are met. For example, a permit rule may grant access to users with a specific claim value or attribute.

Deny Rules: Deny rules explicitly deny access to resources if certain conditions are met. These rules are used to enforce access restrictions based on specific criteria.

Configuring Claims Authorization Rules: Configuring claims authorization rules in AD FS involves the following steps:

Create Permit Rule: Use the **Add-AdfsAuthorizationPolicyRule** CLI command to add a new permit rule that grants access based on specified conditions.

mathematicaCopy code

Add-AdfsAuthorizationPolicyRule -Name "PermitRule" - ClaimType "http://schemas.microsoft.com/ws/2008/06/identity/claims /role" -Value "Admin"

Create Deny Rule: Use the **Add-AdfsAuthorizationPolicyRule** CLI command to add a new deny rule that denies access based on specified conditions.

```mathematica
mathematicaCopy code
Add-AdfsAuthorizationPolicyRule  -Name  "DenyRule"  -
ClaimType
"http://schemas.microsoft.com/ws/2008/06/identity/claims
/role" -Value "Guest"
```

Best Practices for Trust Relationships and Claims Authorization Rules:

Regular Monitoring and Review: Periodically review trust relationships and claims authorization rules to ensure they align with organizational security policies and requirements.

Implement Least Privilege: Apply the principle of least privilege when configuring claims authorization rules to minimize the risk of unauthorized access.

Audit Logging: Enable audit logging for trust relationships and claims authorization rules to track changes and detect potential security incidents.

Testing and Validation: Test trust relationships and claims authorization rules in a controlled environment before deploying them in production to verify their effectiveness and mitigate potential risks.

In summary, configuring trust relationships and claims authorization rules is essential for establishing secure authentication and access control mechanisms in AD FS deployments. By understanding the different types of trust relationships, implementing appropriate configuration settings, and following best practices for managing claims authorization rules, organizations can effectively control access to resources and protect sensitive data from unauthorized access or misuse. Leveraging CLI commands streamlines the configuration process and facilitates efficient management of trust relationships and claims authorization rules within AD FS environments.

Chapter 9: Implementing Secure LDAP (LDAPS) and SSL/TLS

In today's interconnected digital landscape, ensuring secure communication protocols within Active Directory environments is paramount to safeguarding sensitive data, protecting against cyber threats, and maintaining regulatory compliance. Active Directory, Microsoft's directory service, relies on various communication protocols to facilitate interactions between domain controllers, clients, and other network resources. This chapter explores the importance of configuring secure communication protocols within Active Directory and provides practical guidance on deploying these protocols using command-line interface (CLI) commands.

Understanding Communication Protocols in Active Directory: Active Directory utilizes several communication protocols to facilitate interactions between domain controllers and clients. These protocols include:

LDAP (Lightweight Directory Access Protocol): LDAP is the primary protocol used for querying and modifying directory services data within Active Directory.

Kerberos: Kerberos is an authentication protocol that enables secure authentication between clients and domain controllers.

NTLM (NT LAN Manager): NTLM is an authentication protocol used in legacy systems for backward compatibility.

RPC (Remote Procedure Call): RPC is a communication protocol used for client-server communication within Windows environments.

LDAPS (LDAP over SSL/TLS): LDAPS encrypts LDAP traffic using SSL/TLS, providing an additional layer of security for directory service communication.

Importance of Secure Communication Protocols: Configuring secure communication protocols within Active Directory is essential for several reasons:

Data Confidentiality: Secure communication protocols, such as LDAPS, encrypt data in transit, ensuring confidentiality and preventing unauthorized access.

Authentication Security: Protocols like Kerberos offer strong authentication mechanisms, reducing the risk of credential theft or unauthorized access.

Compliance Requirements: Many regulatory standards, such as GDPR or HIPAA, mandate the use of secure communication protocols to protect sensitive information and ensure data privacy.

Protection Against Threats: Secure protocols mitigate the risk of eavesdropping, man-in-the-middle attacks, and other security threats that exploit unencrypted communication channels.

Deploying LDAPS (LDAP over SSL/TLS): LDAPS encrypts LDAP traffic using SSL/TLS, providing enhanced security for directory service communication. To deploy LDAPS in Active Directory, follow these steps:

Install SSL/TLS Certificate: Obtain or generate an SSL/TLS certificate for the domain controller.

Enable LDAPS: Use the **certutil** command to install and configure the SSL/TLS certificate for LDAPS:

swiftCopy code

```
certutil -f -dspublish "C:\path\to\certificate.crt" RootCA
```

Configure LDAP Service: Modify the LDAP service settings to enable LDAPS on the domain controller:

```
Copy code
dsconfigldap -enablessl
```

Enabling SMB Signing: Server Message Block (SMB) signing helps prevent man-in-the-middle attacks by digitally signing SMB packets. To enable SMB signing in Active Directory, use the following command:

```
mathematicaCopy code
Set-ItemProperty                    -Path
"HKLM:\SYSTEM\CurrentControlSet\Services\LanmanServ
er\Parameters" RequireSecuritySignature -Value 1
```

Implementing IPsec for Network Communication: Internet Protocol Security (IPsec) provides network-level authentication and encryption, securing communication between domain controllers and clients. To configure IPsec policies in Active Directory, use the following command:

```
sqlCopy code
netsh advfirewall consec add rule name="IPsec Policy"
dir=in action=block protocol=ANY
```

Monitoring Communication Protocols: Regular monitoring of communication protocols is crucial for identifying security vulnerabilities, detecting anomalous behavior, and ensuring compliance with security policies. Tools such as Wireshark or Microsoft Network Monitor can be used to capture and analyze network traffic for signs of unauthorized access or suspicious activity.

Best Practices for Secure Communication:

Regular Updates: Keep systems and protocols up-to-date with the latest security patches and updates to address known vulnerabilities.

Implement Encryption: Encrypt sensitive data at rest and in transit using robust encryption algorithms to prevent unauthorized access.

Strong Authentication: Enforce strong authentication mechanisms, such as multi-factor authentication (MFA), to verify the identity of users and devices accessing the network.

Access Control: Implement access control policies to restrict access to sensitive resources based on user roles, permissions, and organizational policies.

In summary, configuring secure communication protocols is essential for ensuring the confidentiality, integrity, and availability of data within Active Directory environments. By deploying protocols such as LDAPS, enabling SMB signing, and implementing IPsec for network communication, organizations can strengthen their security posture and mitigate the risk of data breaches and cyber attacks. Leveraging CLI commands streamlines the deployment process and facilitates efficient management of communication protocols within Active Directory environments.

In the realm of network security, establishing secure communication channels is imperative to safeguard sensitive data and thwart potential threats. When it comes to Active Directory, deploying SSL/TLS certificates for LDAPS (LDAP over SSL/TLS) encryption is a crucial step in fortifying the integrity of directory services. This chapter delves into the intricacies of deploying SSL/TLS certificates for LDAPS encryption, providing practical insights and CLI commands for seamless implementation.

Understanding LDAPS Encryption: LDAPS encryption augments the security of LDAP communication by encrypting data transmitted between LDAP clients and servers using SSL/TLS protocols. By implementing LDAPS, organizations can protect sensitive information from unauthorized access and interception, thereby bolstering the confidentiality and integrity of directory services.

Obtaining SSL/TLS Certificates: The first step in deploying LDAPS encryption is to procure SSL/TLS certificates from a trusted Certificate Authority (CA). Organizations can choose between self-signed certificates for internal use or acquire certificates from reputable third-party CAs for enhanced trust and validation.

Generating Self-Signed Certificates: To generate a self-signed SSL/TLS certificate for LDAPS encryption, administrators can utilize the **New-SelfSignedCertificate** cmdlet in Windows PowerShell. The following command generates a self-signed certificate with specified parameters:

```sql
sqlCopy code
New-SelfSignedCertificate            -DnsName
"ldap.example.com"          -CertStoreLocation
"Cert:\LocalMachine\My"
```

Requesting Certificates from Public CAs: For external-facing LDAPS implementations or scenarios requiring enhanced trust, organizations can request SSL/TLS certificates from public CAs. This process typically involves submitting a Certificate Signing Request (CSR) generated on the server to the CA, who then issues a signed certificate.

Installing Certificates on Domain Controllers: Once SSL/TLS certificates are obtained, administrators must install them on the domain controllers hosting Active Directory services. This can be achieved using the

Certificate Management snap-in (**certlm.msc**) or PowerShell commands such as **Import-Certificate**.

Configuring LDAPS: After installing SSL/TLS certificates, LDAPS must be configured on the domain controllers to utilize the certificates for encryption. This involves enabling LDAPS and specifying the certificate to be used for SSL/TLS encryption. The following command enables LDAPS on a domain controller:

Copy code

ldifde -f ldapsenable.txt

Testing LDAPS Connectivity: It's imperative to verify the functionality of LDAPS encryption after configuration. Administrators can test LDAPS connectivity using tools like LDP.exe or PowerShell. The following PowerShell command initiates an LDAPS connection to a specified domain controller:

csharpCopy code

[System.DirectoryServices.Protocols.LdapConnection]::new("dc.example.com",636)

Renewing and Managing Certificates: SSL/TLS certificates have finite lifespans and must be renewed periodically to ensure uninterrupted LDAPS encryption. Administrators should establish procedures for certificate renewal and monitor expiration dates to avoid service disruptions. Tools like PowerShell's **Get-ChildItem** cmdlet can be leveraged to manage certificate expiration.

Implementing Certificate Revocation: In cases where SSL/TLS certificates are compromised or no longer trusted, administrators must promptly revoke them to prevent unauthorized usage. This can be accomplished using the Certificate Authority's management interface or PowerShell cmdlets such as **Revoke-Certificate**.

Best Practices for LDAPS Certificate Management:

Certificate Rotation: Regularly rotate SSL/TLS certificates to mitigate the risk of exploitation and maintain compliance with security standards.

Centralized Management: Utilize centralized certificate management solutions to streamline certificate provisioning, monitoring, and renewal processes.

Secure Key Storage: Safeguard private keys associated with SSL/TLS certificates by storing them in secure, encrypted repositories to prevent unauthorized access.

In summary, deploying SSL/TLS certificates for LDAPS encryption is a fundamental aspect of securing Active Directory environments. By following best practices, implementing robust certificate management processes, and leveraging CLI commands for configuration and testing, organizations can establish resilient LDAPS encryption mechanisms to safeguard their directory services against malicious threats.

Chapter 10: Responding to Active Directory Security Incidents

In today's dynamic and ever-evolving cyber threat landscape, organizations must be prepared to effectively respond to security incidents to mitigate potential damages and minimize disruptions to their operations. Incident response planning and procedures play a pivotal role in enabling organizations to swiftly detect, contain, eradicate, and recover from security breaches. This chapter explores the importance of incident response planning and outlines essential procedures, along with CLI commands where applicable, to facilitate a robust incident response framework.

Understanding Incident Response: Incident response refers to the systematic approach taken by organizations to manage and address security incidents promptly and effectively. These incidents can range from cyber attacks and data breaches to insider threats and system vulnerabilities. The primary goals of incident response are to limit the impact of incidents, restore normal operations, and prevent future occurrences.

Key Components of Incident Response Planning:

Preparation: This phase involves developing comprehensive incident response plans, establishing incident response teams, and conducting regular training and drills to ensure readiness.

Detection and Analysis: Organizations must deploy monitoring tools and mechanisms to detect and analyze potential security incidents in real-time, allowing for swift identification and classification.

Containment and Eradication: Once an incident is confirmed, immediate action must be taken to contain its spread and eradicate the underlying threat to prevent further damage.

Recovery: Following containment, organizations must focus on restoring affected systems and data to their pre-incident state, ensuring minimal disruption to business operations.

Post-Incident Analysis: After resolving the incident, a thorough post-mortem analysis should be conducted to assess the effectiveness of the response efforts, identify areas for improvement, and update incident response plans accordingly.

Developing an Incident Response Plan (IRP):

Identification of Stakeholders: Identify key stakeholders and members of the incident response team, including IT personnel, security analysts, legal advisors, and senior management.

Risk Assessment: Conduct a comprehensive risk assessment to identify potential threats, vulnerabilities, and critical assets that may be targeted by attackers.

Defining Incident Severity Levels: Establish clear criteria for categorizing and prioritizing incidents based on their severity and potential impact on the organization.

Incident Handling Procedures: Document detailed procedures for responding to various types of incidents, including steps for containment, eradication, recovery, and communication.

Communication Plan: Define communication protocols for notifying internal stakeholders, external partners, regulatory authorities, and law enforcement agencies in the event of a security incident.

Regular Testing and Review: Regularly test and update the incident response plan through tabletop exercises, simulated drills, and post-incident reviews to ensure its effectiveness and relevance.

CLI Commands for Incident Response:

Network Traffic Analysis: Tools like Wireshark or tcpdump can be used to capture and analyze network traffic for signs of suspicious activity. Example command:

cssCopy code

tcpdump -i eth0 -w capture.pcap

System Log Analysis: Use the **grep** command in Unix/Linux environments or **Select-String** cmdlet in PowerShell to search system logs for indicators of compromise (IOCs). Example command:

cCopy code

grep "Failed login attempt" /var/log/auth.log

Endpoint Forensics: Conduct forensic analysis on compromised endpoints using tools like Autopsy or The Sleuth Kit. Example command:

bashCopy code

autopsy -d /path/to/evidence

Executing Incident Response Procedures:

Containment: Upon detection of a security incident, isolate affected systems or segments of the network to prevent further propagation of the threat.

Eradication: Utilize threat intelligence feeds and security tools to identify and remove malicious entities from compromised systems, including malware, backdoors, and unauthorized accounts.

Recovery: Restore affected systems and data from backups, applying necessary patches and security updates to prevent re-infection.

Communication: Maintain transparent communication with internal stakeholders, customers, and regulatory bodies throughout the incident response process, providing regular updates on the situation and mitigation efforts.

Post-Incident Analysis and Lessons Learned:

Root Cause Analysis: Conduct a thorough investigation to identify the root causes of the incident, including any gaps in security controls or procedural deficiencies.

Documentation: Document key findings, lessons learned, and recommendations for improving incident response capabilities in the future.

Continuous Improvement: Implement corrective actions and enhancements to incident response plans, processes, and technologies based on the insights gained from the post-incident analysis.

Best Practices for Incident Response:

Proactive Monitoring: Deploy advanced threat detection tools and techniques to proactively monitor for signs of anomalous behavior and potential security incidents.

Collaboration and Coordination: Foster collaboration between internal teams, external partners, and industry peers to share threat intelligence and best practices for incident response.

Regular Training and Drills: Conduct regular training exercises and simulated incident response drills to ensure that personnel are prepared to effectively respond to security incidents in real-world scenarios.

In summary, incident response planning and procedures are critical components of a comprehensive cybersecurity strategy. By following best practices, documenting incident response plans, and leveraging CLI commands for efficient execution, organizations can enhance their ability to detect, respond to, and recover from security incidents, thereby safeguarding their assets and preserving business continuity.

Detecting and mitigating Active Directory (AD) security breaches is paramount in safeguarding organizational data and infrastructure from malicious actors. Active Directory, as the central identity management system in many environments, is a prime target for cyber attacks due to its critical role in managing user accounts, permissions, and access controls. This chapter delves into the strategies and techniques for detecting and mitigating security breaches within Active Directory environments, along with practical CLI commands and deployment methods.

Understanding AD Security Breaches: Active Directory security breaches encompass a wide range of malicious activities, including unauthorized access, privilege escalation, data exfiltration, and lateral movement. These breaches can result from various attack vectors, such as credential theft, phishing, malware infections, and misconfigured permissions.

Signs of AD Security Breaches:

Unusual login attempts or access patterns detected in authentication logs.

Anomalous changes to user permissions, group memberships, or Group Policy settings.

Abnormal activity in domain controller event logs, such as failed authentication events or unusual service modifications.

Presence of suspicious files, processes, or registry entries on domain-joined systems indicating potential compromise.

Detecting AD Security Breaches:

Audit Logging: Enable comprehensive auditing in Active Directory to track critical events and changes. Use the **auditpol** command in Windows Server to configure audit policies:

bashCopy code

```
auditpol /set /subcategory:"Directory Service Changes" /success:enable /failure:enable
```

Security Information and Event Management (SIEM): Implement a SIEM solution to centralize log collection, correlation, and analysis from various AD components and endpoints.

Endpoint Detection and Response (EDR): Deploy EDR agents on domain-joined systems to monitor for suspicious behavior and indicators of compromise (IOCs).

Mitigating AD Security Breaches:

Isolation: Immediately isolate compromised systems or accounts from the network to prevent further damage or unauthorized access.

Password Resets: Reset passwords for potentially compromised user accounts and service accounts to prevent unauthorized access.

Privilege Revocation: Revoke unnecessary privileges and group memberships from compromised accounts to limit the scope of the breach.

Patch Management: Ensure all systems and applications are promptly patched with the latest security updates to address known vulnerabilities exploited by attackers.

CLI Commands for Breach Detection and Mitigation:

Lockout Status of User Accounts:

javascriptCopy code

```
net user <username> /domain | findstr /C:"Account Lockout Threshold"
```

Force Password Reset:

bashCopy code

```
net user <username> /domain /passwordreq:yes
```

Check Group Memberships:

bashCopy code

```
net group "Domain Admins" /domain
```

Review Security Logs:

mathematicaCopy code

```
Get-EventLog -LogName Security -InstanceId <EventID> -Newest <Number>
```

Incident Response Workflow:

Detection: Rapidly detect and triage security incidents through real-time monitoring and analysis of AD logs and network traffic.

Containment: Immediately contain the breach by isolating affected systems or segments of the network to prevent further spread.

Investigation: Conduct a thorough investigation to determine the root cause, extent of the breach, and impact on critical assets.

Remediation: Take proactive measures to remediate the breach, including patching vulnerabilities, resetting compromised credentials, and removing malicious artifacts.

Communication: Maintain transparent communication with stakeholders, including IT teams, management, legal counsel, and law enforcement agencies, throughout the incident response process.

Continuous Improvement:

Post-Incident Analysis: Conduct a comprehensive post-mortem analysis to identify lessons learned, gaps in security controls, and areas for improvement in incident response procedures.

Security Awareness Training: Educate employees on common attack vectors, phishing techniques, and best practices for maintaining secure credentials to prevent future breaches.

In summary, detecting and mitigating Active Directory security breaches requires a proactive approach, robust monitoring capabilities, and swift incident response procedures. By leveraging CLI commands, implementing effective detection mechanisms, and following established incident response workflows, organizations can effectively protect their AD environments from evolving cyber threats and minimize the impact of security breaches on their operations and data.

BOOK 4
ACTIVE DIRECTORY TROUBLESHOOTING AND OPTIMIZATION
EXPERT TIPS FOR PEAK PERFORMANCE AND RESILIENCE

ROB BOTWRIGHT

Chapter 1: Understanding Active Directory Architecture

Active Directory (AD) is a fundamental component of the Windows operating system family, serving as a centralized directory service for managing users, computers, groups, and other network resources within a Windows domain environment. Understanding the components and architecture of Active Directory is essential for system administrators and IT professionals tasked with deploying, managing, and maintaining AD infrastructure. This chapter explores the key components and concepts of Active Directory, along with practical CLI commands and deployment techniques.

Active Directory Domains: An Active Directory domain is a logical grouping of network resources, including users, computers, and devices, that share a common directory database and security policies. Domains establish boundaries for security and administrative purposes, enabling centralized management of resources within the domain. Administrators can use the dcpromo command in Windows Server to promote a server to a domain controller and create a new domain.

Active Directory Forests: A forest is a collection of one or more Active Directory domains that share a common schema, configuration, and global catalog. Forests enable organizations to establish trust relationships between domains and provide a hierarchical structure for organizing directory information. To create a new forest, administrators can use the dcpromo command with the /forestprep and /domainprep options to prepare the schema and domain for installation.

Domain Controllers (DCs): Domain controllers are servers running the Windows Server operating system that store a copy of the Active Directory database and are responsible for authenticating and authorizing users and computers within the domain. Administrators can use the dcpromo command to promote a server to a domain controller role.

Active Directory Sites: Active Directory sites represent physical or logical network locations that facilitate efficient replication of directory information between domain controllers. Sites help optimize network traffic and ensure fault tolerance by defining replication boundaries based on network connectivity and bandwidth. Administrators can use the dssite command-line tool to manage Active Directory sites, subnets, and site links.

Organizational Units (OUs): Organizational units are containers within Active Directory domains used to organize and manage objects, such as users, groups, and computers, in a hierarchical structure. OUs provide granularity for applying Group Policy settings, delegating administrative authority, and simplifying management tasks. Administrators can use the dsacls command-line tool to manage permissions on OUs and their contents.

Group Policy Objects (GPOs): Group Policy objects are collections of settings that define the configuration and security policies applied to users and computers within an Active Directory domain. GPOs enable administrators to enforce uniform settings, such as password policies, software restrictions, and desktop configurations, across the domain. Administrators can use the gpedit.msc or gpupdate command-line tool to manage and apply Group Policy settings.

Global Catalog Servers: Global catalog servers are domain controllers that maintain a partial replica of all objects in the forest, providing comprehensive search capabilities and

239

facilitating user authentication and resource access across domains. Administrators can use the ntdsutil command-line tool to manage the global catalog and perform operations, such as forcing a server to become a global catalog or verifying the global catalog configuration.

Active Directory Schema: The Active Directory schema defines the structure and attributes of objects stored in the directory, including users, groups, and computers. The schema is extensible, allowing administrators to customize and extend the directory schema to accommodate specific organizational requirements. To manage the Active Directory schema, administrators can use the ldifde or dsquery command-line tools to import or export schema definitions and attributes.

In summary, Active Directory is a complex directory service comprising multiple components and concepts that work together to provide centralized identity and access management in Windows environments. By understanding the roles and functions of each component, administrators can effectively design, deploy, and manage Active Directory infrastructure to meet the needs of their organization's IT environment.

Domain, forest, and trust relationships are fundamental concepts in the architecture of Active Directory, the directory service provided by Microsoft Windows Server operating systems. Understanding these concepts is essential for designing and managing complex network infrastructures effectively. This chapter explores the definitions, deployment techniques, and CLI commands associated with domain, forest, and trust relationships.

1. Domain: A domain in Active Directory represents a logical grouping of network resources, including users, computers, and devices, that share a common directory database and security policies. Each domain has its own unique domain name and is administered as a separate entity within an Active Directory environment. To create a new domain, administrators typically use the **dcpromo** command-line tool in Windows Server. For example, to promote a server named DC1 to a domain controller for the domain example.com, the following command can be used:

bashCopy code

```
dcpromo /unattend /replicaOrNewDomain:domain
/newDomain:forest /newDomainDNSName:example.com
/domainNetbiosName:EXAMPLE /forestLevel:4
/domainLevel:4 /safeModeAdminPassword:Pa$$w0rd
/databasePath:"D:\NTDS" /logPath:"D:\NTDSLogs"
/sysvolpath:"D:\Sysvol" /rebootOnCompletion:Yes
```

2. Forest: A forest is a collection of one or more Active Directory domains that share a common schema, configuration, and global catalog. It represents the highest level of organization within an Active Directory infrastructure and provides a security boundary for authentication and resource access. Deploying a new forest involves promoting the first domain controller in a new domain or creating a new domain tree within an existing forest. Administrators can use the **dcpromo** command with the **/forestprep** and **/domainprep** options to prepare the schema and domain for installation in a new forest.

3. Trust Relationships: Trust relationships establish secure communication channels between domains or forests, enabling users in one domain to access resources in another domain. There are two main types of trust relationships: one-way trusts and two-way trusts. In a one-way trust, authentication requests flow in one direction only, whereas in a two-way trust, authentication requests flow in both directions. Trusts can be created manually using the Active

Directory Domains and Trusts console or using the **Netdom** command-line tool. For example, to create a two-way trust between two domains, the following command can be used: phpCopy code

Netdom trust <TrustingDomainName> /Domain:<TrustedDomainName> /TwoWay /UserD:<DomainAdmin> /PasswordD:<AdminPassword> /UserO:<TrustedDomainAdmin> /PasswordO:<TrustedAdminPassword>

4. Transitive Trusts: Active Directory trusts are transitive by default, meaning that if Domain A trusts Domain B and Domain B trusts Domain C, then Domain A implicitly trusts Domain C. This transitivity simplifies trust management and enables users to access resources across multiple domains without requiring separate trust relationships for each domain pair.

5. Trust Verification: Administrators can verify trust relationships using various CLI commands, such as **nltest** and **Test-ComputerSecureChannel** in PowerShell. These commands allow administrators to check the status of trust relationships, troubleshoot authentication issues, and ensure the integrity of communication channels between domains and forests.

In summary, domain, forest, and trust relationships are core concepts in Active Directory architecture, providing the foundation for centralized identity and access management in Windows environments. By understanding how to deploy and manage these relationships using CLI commands and administrative tools, administrators can design robust and secure Active Directory infrastructures that meet the needs of their organizations.

Chapter 2: Common Active Directory Performance Issues

Identifying bottlenecks and performance degradation is crucial for maintaining optimal performance in Active Directory environments. When users experience slow logon times, delays in accessing resources, or general system sluggishness, administrators must quickly diagnose and address underlying issues to ensure smooth operation. This chapter explores various techniques, tools, and CLI commands for identifying and resolving bottlenecks and performance degradation in Active Directory.

1. Performance Monitoring: Performance monitoring is a proactive approach to identifying potential bottlenecks before they impact system performance. Administrators can use the built-in Performance Monitor tool (**perfmon**) in Windows Server to collect and analyze performance data over time. By monitoring key performance counters related to CPU usage, memory utilization, disk I/O, and network traffic, administrators can identify trends and anomalies that may indicate performance issues.

2. Resource Utilization Analysis: Resource utilization analysis involves assessing the usage of hardware resources such as CPU, memory, disk, and network bandwidth. CLI commands such as **Task Manager**, **System Monitor**, and **Resource Monitor** provide real-time visibility into resource consumption by processes and services running on domain controllers. By identifying processes that consume excessive resources, administrators can take corrective actions to optimize system performance.

3. Active Directory Performance Counters: Active Directory exposes a set of performance counters that provide insights into the health and performance of domain controllers.

Administrators can use the **Perfmon** tool to monitor Active Directory performance counters such as LDAP operations/sec, DRA Pending Replication Synchronizations, and Database Page Fault Stalls/sec. By tracking these counters, administrators can identify performance bottlenecks related to LDAP queries, replication latency, and database operations.

4. Replication Monitoring: Replication latency and backlog can significantly impact the performance of Active Directory environments, especially in multi-site deployments. Administrators can use the **Repadmin** command-line tool to monitor replication status, view replication metadata, and troubleshoot replication issues. For example, the following command can be used to check the replication status between two domain controllers:

```php
phpCopy code
Repadmin /showrepl <SourceDomainController> <DestinationDomainController>
```

5. Log Analysis: Active Directory domain controllers generate event logs that contain valuable information about system events, errors, and warnings. Administrators can use the Event Viewer (**eventvwr**) tool to analyze event logs and identify potential causes of performance degradation. By filtering event logs based on specific event IDs or error codes, administrators can pinpoint issues related to authentication failures, DNS resolution errors, and replication problems.

6. Performance Testing and Benchmarking: Performance testing involves simulating real-world scenarios to evaluate the scalability and responsiveness of Active Directory infrastructure. Administrators can use tools like **LoadGen** (Load Generator) to generate simulated workloads and measure system performance under varying levels of load.

By conducting performance tests and benchmarks, administrators can identify bottlenecks, fine-tune system configurations, and optimize resource allocation to improve overall performance.

7. Capacity Planning: Capacity planning involves forecasting future resource requirements based on current usage trends and anticipated growth. Administrators can use performance data collected from monitoring tools to identify capacity constraints and plan for hardware upgrades or additional resources as needed. By proactively addressing capacity issues, administrators can ensure that Active Directory environments can scale to meet the demands of growing workloads and user populations.

In summary, identifying bottlenecks and performance degradation in Active Directory requires a combination of proactive monitoring, performance analysis, and troubleshooting techniques. By leveraging CLI commands, performance counters, event logs, and testing tools, administrators can effectively diagnose performance issues, implement corrective actions, and maintain optimal performance in Active Directory environments.

Performance optimization is a critical aspect of managing Active Directory environments to ensure efficient operation and responsiveness. Next, we'll explore various strategies and techniques for optimizing the performance of Active Directory.

1. Indexing and Search Optimization: Indexing plays a crucial role in improving the performance of LDAP queries and searches in Active Directory. Administrators can optimize search performance by creating appropriate indexes on attributes commonly used in search filters. The **ldifde** command-line tool can be used to export schema information, including indexed attributes. For example, to export schema information to an LDIF file, you can use the following command:

graphqlCopy code

```
ldifde          -f          schema.ldf          -d
"cn=schema,cn=configuration,dc=domain,dc=com"
```

Once exported, administrators can review the schema information to identify attributes that require indexing and use the **ntdsutil** tool to create or remove indexes accordingly.

2. DNS Configuration and Optimization: DNS plays a crucial role in Active Directory authentication and name resolution. Optimizing DNS configuration involves ensuring that domain controllers are correctly registered in DNS and that DNS queries are efficiently resolved. Administrators can use the **nslookup** command-line tool to troubleshoot DNS resolution issues and verify DNS records. For example, the following command can be used to query DNS records for a specific domain controller:

phpCopy code

```
nslookup <domain_controller_name>
```

Additionally, configuring DNS forwarders and implementing DNS caching can help reduce the latency of DNS queries and improve overall network performance.

3. Replication Optimization: Optimizing Active Directory replication is essential for ensuring timely and efficient data synchronization between domain controllers. Administrators can optimize replication by configuring appropriate replication intervals, site link costs, and replication schedules. The **repadmin** command-line tool can be used to monitor replication status, force replication between domain controllers, and troubleshoot replication issues. For example, the following command can be used to force replication from a source domain controller to a destination domain controller:

bashCopy code

repadmin /syncall <DestinationDomainController> /APed

Additionally, implementing Read-Only Domain Controllers (RODCs) in branch offices can help reduce replication traffic and improve performance by providing local authentication and directory services.

4. Group Policy Optimization: Group Policy processing can impact system startup and logon times in Active Directory environments. Administrators can optimize Group Policy processing by minimizing the number of GPOs applied to users and computers, avoiding unnecessary settings, and organizing GPOs into logical containers. The **gpresult** and **rsop.msc** command-line tools can be used to diagnose Group Policy processing issues and identify the applied GPOs and settings. For example, the following command can be used to generate a Group Policy Result report for a specific user or computer:

bashCopy code

gpresult /user <username> /scope computer /v

5. Active Directory Database Maintenance: Regular maintenance of the Active Directory database is essential for optimizing performance and preventing database fragmentation. Administrators can perform database maintenance tasks such as offline defragmentation (**ntdsutil**) and database integrity checks (**esentutl**) to ensure database consistency and optimize storage utilization. Additionally, monitoring database growth and implementing proper disk storage solutions can help prevent performance degradation due to disk space constraints.

6. Hardware and Resource Scaling: Scaling hardware resources such as CPU, memory, disk, and network bandwidth can significantly improve the performance of Active Directory environments, especially in large or high-traffic deployments. Administrators should regularly assess resource utilization and scalability requirements and upgrade hardware components as needed to meet growing demands. Virtualization technologies such as Hyper-V and VMware can also be used to dynamically allocate resources and optimize hardware utilization.

7. Performance Monitoring and Tuning: Continuous performance monitoring and tuning are essential for maintaining optimal performance in Active Directory environments. Administrators should regularly monitor performance metrics such as CPU usage, memory utilization, disk I/O, and network latency using built-in performance monitoring tools (**perfmon**) and third-party monitoring solutions. By analyzing performance data and identifying bottlenecks, administrators can implement targeted optimizations to improve system performance and responsiveness.

In summary, optimizing performance in Active Directory requires a combination of proactive monitoring, configuration tuning, and resource management techniques. By implementing strategies such as indexing and search optimization, DNS configuration, replication optimization, Group Policy optimization, database maintenance, hardware scaling, and performance monitoring, administrators can ensure that Active Directory environments operate efficiently and deliver optimal performance for users and applications.

Chapter 3: Monitoring Active Directory Health

Active Directory monitoring is crucial for ensuring the health, security, and performance of your directory services. Next, we'll explore various tools and techniques that administrators can use to monitor Active Directory effectively.

1. Performance Monitor (PerfMon): Performance Monitor, also known as PerfMon, is a built-in Windows tool that allows administrators to monitor various performance metrics of the system and applications, including Active Directory. Administrators can use PerfMon to track metrics such as CPU usage, memory utilization, disk I/O, and network traffic. By analyzing these metrics, administrators can identify performance bottlenecks and optimize system resources accordingly.

To launch PerfMon, you can use the **perfmon** command from the command prompt or search for "Performance Monitor" in the Start menu. From the PerfMon interface, you can add counters related to Active Directory, such as LDAP operations, Kerberos authentication, and replication latency, to monitor the health and performance of your directory services.

2. Active Directory Administrative Center (ADAC): Active Directory Administrative Center (ADAC) is a graphical management tool introduced in Windows Server 2008 R2 that provides a centralized interface for managing various aspects of Active Directory. In addition to administration tasks, ADAC also includes built-in monitoring capabilities that allow administrators to view and analyze directory-related events and performance metrics.

To access the monitoring features in ADAC, open the tool from the Administrative Tools menu on a Windows Server machine with the Active Directory Administrative Center feature installed. From the ADAC interface, navigate to the "Monitoring" tab to view real-time and historical data on directory-related events, such as changes to objects, authentication failures, and replication status.

3. Event Viewer: Event Viewer is another built-in Windows tool that administrators can use to monitor and analyze events logged by the operating system and applications, including Active Directory. Event Viewer provides a central repository for viewing event logs from various sources, allowing administrators to track system events, errors, and warnings.

To launch Event Viewer, you can use the **eventvwr.msc** command from the command prompt or search for "Event Viewer" in the Start menu. From the Event Viewer interface, navigate to the "Windows Logs" section and select "Directory Service" to view events related to Active Directory. Administrators can filter events based on severity, source, and event ID to focus on specific issues or activities.

4. PowerShell Monitoring Scripts: PowerShell scripting can be a powerful tool for automating Active Directory monitoring tasks and generating custom reports. Administrators can use PowerShell cmdlets such as **Get-ADDomainController**, **Get-ADReplicationPartnerMetadata**, and **Get-EventLog** to retrieve information about domain controllers, replication status, and directory-related events.

For example, administrators can use the following PowerShell script to retrieve replication status for all domain controllers in a forest:

powershellCopy code

```
Get-ADDomainController -Filter * | ForEach-Object { Get-
ADReplicationPartnerMetadata -Target $($_.Name) -Scope
"Domain" | Select-Object Server, LastReplicationResult }
```

By scheduling these scripts to run periodically, administrators can automate the monitoring process and receive regular reports on the health and performance of their Active Directory environment.

5. Third-Party Monitoring Solutions: In addition to built-in tools, administrators can also leverage third-party monitoring solutions specifically designed for Active Directory monitoring. These solutions offer advanced features such as real-time monitoring, alerting, performance analysis, and historical reporting.

Popular third-party Active Directory monitoring solutions include ManageEngine ADManager Plus, SolarWinds Server & Application Monitor, and Quest Active Administrator. These tools provide comprehensive monitoring capabilities and can help streamline the management of complex Active Directory environments.

In summary, Active Directory monitoring is essential for maintaining the health, security, and performance of your directory services. By using tools such as Performance Monitor, Active Directory Administrative Center, Event Viewer, PowerShell monitoring scripts, and third-party monitoring solutions, administrators can gain insight into the operational status of Active Directory and proactively address any issues or concerns.

Establishing baselines and thresholds is a fundamental aspect of effectively monitoring and managing any system, including Active Directory. Next, we will delve into the importance of establishing baselines and thresholds, the techniques involved, and how administrators can leverage them to ensure the optimal performance and stability of their Active Directory environment.

1. Understanding Baselines: A baseline is a set of reference metrics that represent normal operating conditions for a system over a period of time. Baselines serve as benchmarks against which deviations can be measured and analyzed. In the context of Active Directory, baselines can include metrics such as CPU utilization, memory usage, disk I/O, network traffic, and directory service-specific parameters like LDAP operations and replication latency.

2. Importance of Baselines: Baselines provide administrators with valuable insights into the typical behavior and performance of their Active Directory environment. By establishing baselines for key metrics, administrators can:

Identify deviations from normal behavior that may indicate underlying issues or performance degradation.

Proactively detect potential problems before they escalate into critical issues.

Assess the impact of configuration changes, updates, or new deployments on system performance.

Make informed decisions about resource allocation, capacity planning, and infrastructure upgrades.

3. Techniques for Establishing Baselines: There are several techniques that administrators can use to establish baselines for their Active Directory environment:

Performance Monitoring: Utilize tools such as Performance Monitor (PerfMon) to collect performance data over time and identify trends. Set up counters for relevant metrics such as CPU utilization, memory usage, disk I/O, and LDAP operations, and monitor these metrics regularly to establish baseline values.

Log Analysis: Analyze event logs and diagnostic logs generated by Active Directory components to track system events, errors, and warnings. Look for patterns and anomalies in log data to identify trends and establish baseline behavior.

Historical Data Analysis: Collect historical performance data from previous monitoring sessions and analyze it to identify patterns and trends. By comparing current data to historical data, administrators can detect deviations and establish baseline performance levels.

4. Setting Thresholds: Thresholds are predefined limits or thresholds that indicate when a metric has exceeded acceptable levels and requires attention. Thresholds can be based on performance metrics, such as CPU utilization exceeding 80% or replication latency exceeding 100 milliseconds. Administrators can configure monitoring systems to generate alerts when metrics exceed predefined thresholds, allowing them to take proactive action to address issues.

5. Configuring Threshold Alerts: Most monitoring tools allow administrators to configure threshold alerts based on predefined conditions. For example, administrators can use the following PowerShell command to create a threshold alert for CPU utilization exceeding 80% on a domain controller:

powershellCopy code

```
Set-Counter -Counter "\Processor(_Total)\% Processor Time" -WarningValue 80
```

This command sets a warning threshold of 80% for CPU utilization. When CPU utilization exceeds this threshold, the monitoring system can trigger an alert, allowing administrators to investigate the issue further.

6. Best Practices for Baseline and Threshold Management:
Regularly review and update baselines to account for changes in system configuration, workload, or infrastructure.

Document baseline values and thresholds for key performance metrics to ensure consistency and clarity.

Monitor critical metrics continuously and configure alerts for thresholds that indicate potential issues or performance degradation.

Regularly analyze monitoring data to identify trends, patterns, and anomalies that may require further investigation or action.

Collaborate with stakeholders, such as system administrators, network engineers, and application developers, to ensure alignment on baseline values and threshold settings.

In summary, establishing baselines and thresholds is essential for effective Active Directory monitoring and management. By understanding normal operating conditions, identifying deviations from baseline behavior, and configuring threshold alerts, administrators can proactively manage their Active Directory environment and ensure optimal performance, stability, and reliability.

Chapter 4: Identifying and Resolving Replication Problems

Troubleshooting replication latency and failures in Active Directory is crucial for maintaining the integrity and consistency of directory data across domain controllers. Replication ensures that changes made to one domain controller are propagated to others in the domain or forest, allowing for consistent directory information and authentication services. However, replication issues can arise due to various factors such as network connectivity problems, Active Directory database corruption, configuration errors, or domain controller hardware failures. Next, we will explore common replication issues, diagnostic techniques, and remediation strategies to address replication latency and failures effectively.

1. Understanding Replication Latency: Replication latency refers to the time it takes for changes made to Active Directory objects on one domain controller to be replicated to other domain controllers within the same replication scope. In an ideal scenario, replication latency should be minimal, ensuring that directory updates are propagated promptly across the entire domain or forest. However, latency can occur due to factors such as network congestion, high server load, or replication topology issues.

2. Identifying Replication Issues: Detecting replication issues requires monitoring replication status and event logs on domain controllers. Administrators can use the following CLI command to check replication status:

powershellCopy code

repadmin /replsummary

This command provides a summary of replication status for all domain controllers in the forest, including the number of successful and failed replications. Additionally, administrators can review event logs, specifically the Directory Service and DFS Replication logs, for replication-related errors and warnings.

3. Troubleshooting Techniques: When troubleshooting replication latency and failures, administrators can employ various diagnostic techniques:

Check Network Connectivity: Verify network connectivity between domain controllers by using tools like ping or PowerShell's Test-NetConnection cmdlet.

Review Replication Topology: Examine the replication topology to ensure proper connectivity between domain controllers. Use the Active Directory Sites and Services console or PowerShell cmdlets like Get-ADReplicationSite and Get-ADReplicationSiteLink to review replication topology configuration.

Validate DNS Configuration: Ensure that DNS records for domain controllers are accurate and up-to-date. Use the nslookup command to verify DNS resolution and troubleshoot any DNS-related issues.

Monitor Replication Status: Continuously monitor replication status using tools like repadmin or Active Directory Replication Status Tool (ADREPLSTATUS) to detect replication failures or backlogs.

4. Remediation Strategies: Once replication issues are identified, administrators can implement remediation strategies to address them:

Resolve Network Issues: Troubleshoot and resolve any network connectivity problems that may be impacting replication. This may involve resolving DNS issues, optimizing network bandwidth, or addressing firewall rules blocking replication traffic.

Fix Replication Errors: Investigate and resolve replication errors by reviewing event logs and identifying the root cause of replication failures. Common issues include lingering objects, replication conflicts, or insufficient permissions.

Force Replication: Force replication between domain controllers using the repadmin command with the /syncall or /syncnow parameters to expedite the replication process.

Perform Active Directory Database Maintenance: Perform integrity checks and database defragmentation using utilities like ntdsutil to address database corruption issues that may impact replication.

5. Testing and Validation: After implementing remediation measures, it's essential to validate the effectiveness of the changes by monitoring replication status and verifying that replication latency has been reduced. Administrators can use tools like repadmin /replsummary and repadmin /showrepl to verify replication status and troubleshoot any remaining issues.

6. Best Practices for Replication Troubleshooting:

Regularly monitor replication status and event logs to proactively detect and address replication issues.

Document replication topology configuration and troubleshooting procedures to ensure consistency and facilitate future troubleshooting efforts.

Conduct periodic replication tests and validation exercises to verify the integrity and efficiency of replication processes.

Collaborate with network administrators and other IT stakeholders to address underlying network infrastructure issues that may impact replication performance.

In summary, troubleshooting replication latency and failures in Active Directory requires a systematic approach involving network analysis, replication status monitoring, and remediation strategies. By employing diagnostic techniques and best practices, administrators can effectively identify and resolve replication issues, ensuring the reliability and consistency of directory services in their environment.

Implementing replication topology optimization is essential for ensuring efficient and reliable replication of Active Directory data across domain controllers. Replication topology defines the connections and routes through which directory updates are transmitted between domain controllers within a domain or forest. By optimizing replication topology, administrators can minimize latency, reduce network traffic, and enhance overall replication performance. Next, we will explore strategies and techniques for designing and implementing an optimized replication topology in Active Directory.

1. Understanding Replication Topology: Replication topology in Active Directory defines the logical connections between domain controllers within a domain or forest. It consists of replication links, bridgehead servers, and site links, which collectively determine the path of directory updates propagation. Understanding the components of replication topology is crucial for optimizing replication efficiency and minimizing latency.

2. Evaluating Existing Replication Topology: Before optimizing replication topology, it's essential to assess the current configuration and performance of replication links and site links. Administrators can use various CLI commands and tools to gather information about replication topology:

powershellCopy code

Get-ADReplicationSite - Retrieves information about Active Directory sites. Get-ADReplicationSiteLink - Retrieves information about Active Directory site links. Get-ADReplicationConnection - Retrieves information about Active Directory replication connections.

These commands provide details about sites, site links, and replication connections, allowing administrators to evaluate the existing replication topology's effectiveness and identify areas for improvement.

3. Designing an Optimized Replication Topology: Optimizing replication topology involves designing an efficient layout of sites, site links, and bridgehead servers to minimize replication latency and maximize bandwidth utilization. Key considerations for designing an optimized replication topology include:

Site Design: Organize domain controllers into sites based on geographical locations, network connectivity, and replication requirements. Sites should reflect the physical network topology to minimize replication traffic over WAN links.

Site Link Configuration: Configure site links to establish replication connections between sites. Define site link costs based on network bandwidth, latency, and reliability to influence replication traffic routing decisions.

Bridgehead Servers: Designate bridgehead servers within each site to serve as communication endpoints for replication traffic. Bridgehead servers facilitate efficient replication communication between sites by aggregating and forwarding directory updates.

4. Implementing Replication Topology Changes: Once the optimized replication topology is designed, administrators can implement changes using the following steps:

Create and Configure Sites: Use the Active Directory Sites and Services console or PowerShell cmdlets to create sites and configure site link bridges to define site connectivity.

Define Site Links: Create site links to establish connections between sites, specifying appropriate costs and replication schedules based on network characteristics.

Configure Bridgehead Servers: Designate domain controllers as bridgehead servers within each site to manage replication traffic flow. Bridgehead servers should be strategically placed to optimize replication efficiency.

Validate Replication Configuration: After making topology changes, validate the replication configuration using tools like repadmin to ensure that replication connections are established and functioning correctly.

5. Monitoring and Fine-Tuning: Continuous monitoring and fine-tuning of replication topology are essential for maintaining optimal replication performance. Administrators should regularly review replication status, site link utilization, and network bandwidth to identify potential bottlenecks or issues. Adjustments to site link costs, replication schedules, or bridgehead server placement may be necessary to adapt to changes in network infrastructure or replication requirements.

6. Best Practices for Replication Topology Optimization:
Plan replication topology based on network infrastructure, site locations, and replication requirements.

Regularly assess replication performance and topology effectiveness using monitoring tools and diagnostic commands.

Document replication topology design and configuration changes to facilitate troubleshooting and future optimizations.

Collaborate with network administrators to ensure alignment between Active Directory replication topology and network infrastructure design.

In summary, implementing replication topology optimization is essential for ensuring efficient and reliable replication of Active Directory data. By designing and configuring an optimized replication topology based on network infrastructure and replication requirements, administrators can minimize latency, reduce network traffic, and enhance overall replication performance in their Active Directory environment.

Chapter 5: Troubleshooting Authentication and Authorization Errors

Analyzing event logs for authentication issues is a critical aspect of maintaining the security and functionality of an Active Directory environment. Authentication events provide valuable insights into user login attempts, authentication failures, and potential security breaches. By effectively analyzing these event logs, administrators can identify and mitigate authentication issues, enhance security posture, and ensure smooth user access to resources. Next, we will explore techniques and best practices for analyzing event logs to troubleshoot authentication issues in Active Directory.

1. Understanding Authentication Events: Authentication events are logged in the Security event log on domain controllers and member servers whenever users attempt to log in or access network resources. These events include successful and failed authentication attempts, account lockouts, password changes, and other security-related activities. Understanding the different types of authentication events and their significance is essential for effective analysis.

2. Using Event Viewer to View Event Logs: Event Viewer is a built-in Windows tool that allows administrators to view and analyze event logs. To access Event Viewer, follow these steps:

Open Event Viewer by pressing **Win + R** to open the Run dialog, then type **eventvwr.msc** and press Enter.

In Event Viewer, navigate to Windows Logs > Security to view authentication-related events.

3. Identifying Common Authentication Issues: Common authentication issues that can be identified through event log analysis include:

Incorrect credentials: Failed authentication events with event IDs such as 4625 (Logon Failure) indicate incorrect username or password.

Account lockouts: Event ID 4740 (Account Lockout) indicates that the account has been locked out due to multiple failed login attempts.

Expired passwords: Event ID 4768 (Kerberos Authentication Service) indicates a failed password change attempt due to an expired password.

Suspicious activity: Anomalies in authentication events, such as multiple failed login attempts from the same IP address, may indicate brute-force attacks or unauthorized access attempts.

4. Filtering and Searching Event Logs: Event Viewer allows administrators to filter and search event logs to narrow down authentication-related events. Use the Filter Current Log option to specify criteria such as event ID, source, or keywords related to authentication issues. Additionally, the Find option can be used to search for specific terms or phrases within event descriptions.

5. Analyzing Event Details: When analyzing authentication events, pay attention to event details such as:

Event ID: Indicates the type of authentication event (e.g., logon failure, account lockout).

Account Name: Specifies the username associated with the authentication attempt.

Logon Type: Indicates the type of logon (e.g., interactive, network).

Failure Reason: Provides information about the reason for authentication failure (e.g., bad password, account locked out).

6. Correlating Events and Troubleshooting Steps: Correlating authentication events with other security-related events can provide valuable context for troubleshooting authentication issues. For example, correlating failed login attempts with account lockout events can help identify the source of authentication failures. Troubleshooting steps may include:

Resetting passwords for locked-out accounts.

Investigating the source of failed login attempts, such as a specific IP address or client device.

Checking for security policy misconfigurations or account permissions issues.

7. Configuring Auditing Policies for Authentication Events: To ensure comprehensive logging of authentication events, configure auditing policies on domain controllers and member servers. Use Group Policy or PowerShell commands to enable auditing of logon events, account lockouts, and other relevant security events. For example, use the following PowerShell command to enable auditing of logon events:

powershellCopy code

```
Set-ItemProperty                -Path
'HKLM:\System\CurrentControlSet\Services\LSA'   -Name
'Audit\AuditLogonEvents' -Value 3
```

8. Regular Monitoring and Review: Regular monitoring and review of authentication event logs are essential for detecting and responding to security incidents in a timely manner. Implement a proactive approach to event log analysis by establishing regular review schedules and leveraging automated monitoring tools to alert administrators to suspicious activity.

In summary, analyzing event logs for authentication issues is a fundamental aspect of maintaining the security and integrity of an Active Directory environment. By understanding authentication events, leveraging event log analysis tools, and implementing proactive monitoring strategies, administrators can effectively troubleshoot authentication issues, mitigate security risks, and ensure secure access to network resources.

Debugging authorization failures in an Active Directory environment is crucial for ensuring that users have appropriate access to resources while maintaining security. Authorization failures occur when users are denied access to resources due to insufficient permissions or misconfigured access controls. Next, we will explore common causes of authorization failures, techniques for debugging these issues, and best practices for resolving them.

1. Understanding Authorization Failures: Authorization failures occur when a user attempts to access a resource, such as a file or folder, and is denied permission to do so. These failures are typically logged in the Security event log on the server hosting the resource. Understanding the various reasons for authorization failures is essential for effective debugging.

2. Analyzing Event Logs for Authorization Failures: Event Viewer is a valuable tool for analyzing authorization failures. To view authorization-related events, navigate to Windows Logs > Security and look for events with event IDs such as 4625 (Logon Failure) and 4656 (Access

Denied). Pay attention to the following details in the event logs:

Account Name: Specifies the username of the user attempting to access the resource.

Object Name: Specifies the name of the resource being accessed.

Access Denied: Indicates that the user was denied access to the resource.

3. Troubleshooting Techniques: When debugging authorization failures, consider the following troubleshooting techniques:

Check Permissions: Verify that the user has the necessary permissions to access the resource. Use the **icacls** command in Command Prompt to view and modify file permissions. For example:

bashCopy code

icacls C:\Path\To\Resource /verify

Review Group Memberships: Ensure that the user is a member of the appropriate security groups that have been granted access to the resource. Use the **net user** and **net group** commands to view user and group memberships. For example:

bashCopy code

net user username net group "Group Name"

Examine ACLs: Review the Access Control Lists (ACLs) associated with the resource to identify any misconfigurations or inconsistencies. Use the **icacls** command to view the ACLs. For example:

bashCopy code

icacls C:\Path\To\Resource /save ACL.txt

Check Group Policy Settings: Review Group Policy settings that may be affecting user access permissions. Use the

Group Policy Management Console (**gpmc.msc**) to examine Group Policy settings applied to the affected user or computer objects.

4. Common Causes of Authorization Failures: Authorization failures can be caused by various factors, including:

Incorrect Permissions: Users may not have the necessary permissions to access the resource.

Group Membership Issues: Users may not be members of the required security groups.

Deny Permissions: Explicit deny permissions may be preventing access to the resource.

Group Policy Restrictions: Group Policy settings may be restricting user access to certain resources.

Network Share Permissions: Permissions on network shares may not be configured correctly.

5. Resolving Authorization Failures: To resolve authorization failures, consider the following steps:

Grant appropriate permissions to the user or relevant security groups.

Ensure that users are members of the correct security groups.

Remove any explicit deny permissions that may be conflicting with allow permissions.

Review and adjust Group Policy settings as needed.

Verify that network share permissions are configured correctly.

6. Testing and Validation: After making changes to address authorization failures, it is essential to test and validate the changes to ensure that users can now access the resource successfully. Use test accounts or test scenarios to verify that the issue has been resolved and that users have the appropriate access permissions.

7. Documenting Changes: Document any changes made to permissions, group memberships, or Group Policy settings to facilitate future troubleshooting and auditing efforts. Maintaining accurate documentation helps ensure consistency and transparency in managing access permissions.

In summary, debugging authorization failures requires a systematic approach that involves analyzing event logs, checking permissions and group memberships, examining ACLs, and reviewing Group Policy settings. By identifying and addressing the root causes of authorization failures, administrators can ensure that users have the appropriate access permissions to resources while maintaining security and compliance with organizational policies.

Chapter 6: Optimizing Active Directory Schema and Global Catalog

Active Directory (AD) Schema forms the foundation of the Active Directory directory service. It defines the structure and attributes of objects stored in the directory. This chapter delves into the fundamental concepts of the AD Schema, its importance, structure, modification procedures, and best practices.

Introduction to Active Directory Schema: The Active Directory Schema is a blueprint that defines the types of objects that can be stored in the directory and their respective attributes. It serves as a template for organizing and managing directory data in a Windows environment.

Schema Components: The AD Schema consists of classes and attributes. Classes define the types of objects (e.g., users, groups, computers) that can be created in the directory, while attributes define the properties of these objects (e.g., name, email address, phone number).

Schema Objects and Attributes: Each object class in the Schema is associated with a set of attributes that describe its properties and characteristics. For example, the user class may have attributes such as "username," "email," and "password."

Schema Partition: The Schema is stored in a dedicated partition within the Active Directory database. This partition is replicated to all domain controllers in the forest and is read-only by default. Modifications to the Schema must be performed with caution.

Extending the Schema: Organizations may need to extend the Schema to accommodate custom applications or additional functionality. This process involves adding new object classes and attributes to the Schema using tools such as "ldifde" or "ldp" (LDAP Data Interchange Format Directory Editor).

bashCopy code

ldifde -i -f schema.ldf

This command imports schema changes from the schema.ldf file into Active Directory.

Schema Management Best Practices: It's essential to follow best practices when managing the AD Schema to ensure stability and consistency:

Document Changes: Document all Schema modifications, including the rationale behind them and potential impacts.

Test Changes: Before making changes to the Schema in a production environment, thoroughly test them in a lab or test environment.

Backup and Recovery: Regularly backup the Schema partition to facilitate recovery in case of errors or unintended changes.

Limit Modifications: Limit Schema modifications to experienced administrators and adhere to change management processes.

Monitor Changes: Implement monitoring mechanisms to track Schema modifications and detect unauthorized changes.

Impact of Schema Changes: Modifying the Schema can have far-reaching effects on the entire Active Directory infrastructure. Changes may affect existing applications, services, and directory-dependent processes. Therefore, it's crucial to assess the impact of Schema changes before implementation.

Rollback Procedures: In case of errors or unforeseen consequences resulting from Schema modifications, it's essential to have rollback procedures in place. This may involve restoring the Schema partition from a backup or reverting specific changes using tools like "ldifde."

bashCopy code

ldifde -i -f rollback.ldf

This command imports the rollback changes from the rollback.ldf file into Active Directory to revert specific modifications.

Schema Versioning: The Schema version indicates the level of compatibility between different versions of Active Directory. It's important to ensure that all domain controllers in the forest are running compatible Schema versions to maintain interoperability.

Active Directory Schema is a critical component of the Windows infrastructure, defining the structure and attributes of directory objects. Understanding its concepts, management procedures, and best practices is essential for maintaining a stable and reliable directory service environment.

In summary, this chapter provides an overview of Active Directory Schema concepts, including its components, management procedures, best practices, and the impact of Schema changes. By understanding these concepts, administrators can effectively manage and maintain the integrity of the Active Directory Schema in their organizations.

The Global Catalog (GC) is a crucial component of the Active Directory (AD) infrastructure, providing a distributed directory service that enables users to efficiently locate resources across domains within a forest.

This chapter explores various techniques for optimizing the Global Catalog to enhance performance, scalability, and reliability in large-scale AD environments.

Understanding the Global Catalog: The Global Catalog is a specialized instance of the AD database that stores a partial replica of all objects in the forest. It contains a subset of attributes for each object and facilitates forest-wide searches for directory information. By default, at least one GC server is present in each AD site.

Identifying Global Catalog Servers: Before optimizing the Global Catalog, it's essential to identify the servers that are hosting GC instances in the environment. This can be done using the "dsquery" command:

bashCopy code

```
dsquery server -forest -isgc
```

This command retrieves a list of all servers in the forest that are hosting Global Catalogs.

Placement of Global Catalog Servers: Strategic placement of GC servers is crucial for optimizing directory access and minimizing latency. GC servers should be distributed across sites to ensure efficient directory searches for users and applications.

GC Replication: GC replication ensures that all GC servers in the forest have consistent directory information. It's essential to monitor and optimize GC replication to prevent replication bottlenecks and ensure timely updates across the forest.

bashCopy code

```
repadmin /showrepl
```

This command displays the replication status of all domain controllers, including GC replication.

Filtering Global Catalog Replication: In large-scale environments, it may be necessary to filter the attributes replicated to the GC to reduce the size of the GC database and improve replication performance. This can be achieved by modifying the "msDS-ReplAttributeMetaData" attribute on the GC server objects.

bashCopy code

```
dsacls                               "CN=NTDS
Settings,CN=Server,CN=Servers,CN=Site,CN=Sites,CN=Conf
iguration,DC=domain,DC=com"   /S  /G  "Authenticated
Users:RPWP;msDS-ReplAttributeMetaData"
```

This command grants the "Authenticated Users" group Read Property with Write Property permissions on the "msDS-ReplAttributeMetaData" attribute, allowing users to modify attribute replication settings.

Optimizing Global Catalog Queries: Efficient use of GC queries is essential for minimizing network traffic and improving query response times. Administrators can optimize GC queries by specifying the required attributes in search filters and limiting the scope of searches to specific GC servers.

GC Load Balancing: Load balancing ensures even distribution of directory queries across multiple GC servers to prevent overloading and performance degradation. This can be achieved using Network Load Balancers (NLB) or DNS round-robin techniques.

Monitoring GC Performance: Regular monitoring of GC performance metrics is crucial for identifying performance bottlenecks and optimizing resource utilization. Key performance indicators include CPU and memory usage, LDAP query response times, and replication latency.

Tuning GC Server Hardware: Adequate hardware resources are essential for optimal GC performance. Administrators should ensure that GC servers are equipped with sufficient CPU, memory, and disk resources to handle directory queries and replication traffic efficiently.

Optimizing the Global Catalog is critical for ensuring efficient directory access and search capabilities in large-scale Active Directory environments. By implementing the techniques outlined Next, administrators can improve GC performance, scalability, and reliability, leading to a more robust and responsive directory service infrastructure.

In summary, this chapter has explored various techniques for optimizing the Global Catalog in Active Directory environments. By understanding the importance of GC optimization and implementing the recommended strategies, administrators can enhance directory performance, scalability, and reliability, ultimately improving the overall user experience and productivity.

Chapter 7: Fine-Tuning Group Policy Performance

Group Policy is a powerful tool used by system administrators to manage user and computer configurations in Active Directory environments. However, delays in Group Policy processing can lead to performance issues and user frustration. This chapter explores common causes of Group Policy processing delays and provides strategies for identifying and resolving these issues.

Understanding Group Policy Processing: Group Policy processing occurs in several stages, including client-side processing (CSP), asynchronous processing, and background processing. Delays in any of these stages can impact the overall time it takes for Group Policy settings to be applied to client computers.

Identifying Group Policy Processing Delays: To diagnose Group Policy processing delays, administrators can use the Group Policy Results Wizard (gpresult) and Group Policy Modeling Wizard in the Group Policy Management Console (GPMC). These tools provide detailed information about applied Group Policy settings and any errors encountered during processing.

bashCopy code

gpresult /r

This command generates a report showing applied Group Policy settings for the current user and computer.

Analyzing Group Policy Event Logs: Event logs on client computers and domain controllers contain valuable information about Group Policy processing events. Administrators can use tools like Event Viewer and PowerShell to analyze Group Policy-related events and identify potential issues.

bashCopy code

Get-WinEvent   -LogName   "Microsoft-Windows-GroupPolicy/Operational"

This PowerShell command retrieves Group Policy-related events from the operational log.

Checking Network Connectivity and Latency: Slow network connectivity or high latency between client computers and domain controllers can cause delays in Group Policy processing. Administrators should use tools like Ping and Tracert to verify network connectivity and identify potential network issues.

bashCopy code

ping <domaincontroller>

This command tests network connectivity to a domain controller.

Reviewing Group Policy Settings: Complex or poorly configured Group Policy settings can result in processing delays. Administrators should review Group Policy settings using tools like the Group Policy Management Console (GPMC) and ensure that policies are organized logically and efficiently.

Optimizing Group Policy Processing: Techniques for optimizing Group Policy processing include using loopback processing, disabling unused Group Policy settings, and leveraging Group Policy caching. These optimizations can help reduce processing times and improve overall system performance.

Resolving DNS Issues: DNS resolution issues can cause delays in Group Policy processing, especially if client computers are unable to resolve domain controller names. Administrators should ensure that DNS settings are correctly configured and that client computers can resolve domain controller names.

bashCopy code

ipconfig /flushdns

This command flushes the DNS resolver cache on a client computer, which can help resolve DNS-related issues.

Testing Group Policy Processing Performance: Administrators can use tools like Group Policy Health to assess the performance of Group Policy processing and identify areas for improvement. These tools provide detailed reports on Group Policy processing times and potential bottlenecks.

Implementing Group Policy Caching: Group Policy caching allows client computers to store Group Policy settings locally, reducing the need for repeated queries to domain controllers. Administrators can enable Group Policy caching through Group Policy settings or registry modifications.

Group Policy processing delays can have a significant impact on system performance and user productivity in Active Directory environments. By following the strategies outlined Next and leveraging diagnostic tools and techniques, administrators can identify and resolve Group Policy processing delays, ensuring efficient and reliable configuration management across the network.

In summary, this chapter has explored various techniques for identifying and resolving Group Policy processing delays in Active Directory environments. By understanding the causes of delays and implementing the recommended strategies, administrators can optimize Group Policy processing and improve overall system performance and user experience.

Group Policy is a powerful tool in the arsenal of system administrators for managing and configuring users' and computers' settings in an Active Directory environment. However, mastering Group Policy goes beyond basic configurations. Next, we delve into advanced Group Policy management strategies that help administrators leverage the full potential of this tool to efficiently manage their network environment.

Understanding Group Policy Inheritance and Precedence: Group Policy settings are applied in a hierarchical manner, with settings inherited from higher-level containers such as the domain, site, or organizational unit (OU). Understanding the order of precedence is crucial for effective Group Policy management. Administrators can use tools like Group Policy Management Console (GPMC) to visualize the inheritance and precedence of Group Policy settings.

bashCopy code

```
gpmc.msc
```

This command opens the Group Policy Management Console, where administrators can view and manage Group Policy objects (GPOs).

Implementing Advanced Group Policy Filtering: Group Policy filtering allows administrators to apply policies selectively based on criteria such as security group membership, WMI filters, or user/device attributes. Advanced filtering techniques enable administrators to target specific users, computers, or groups with granular precision, enhancing the flexibility and efficiency of Group Policy management.

Utilizing Item-Level Targeting (ILT): Item-Level Targeting (ILT) is a feature in Group Policy Preferences that allows administrators to apply settings based on specific conditions such as user or computer attributes, group membership, or registry settings. By using ILT, administrators can tailor Group Policy settings to individual users or computers, providing a more customized and dynamic configuration environment.

Managing Group Policy Preferences: Group Policy Preferences (GPP) extend the capabilities of Group Policy by providing additional configuration options such as drive mappings, folder options, printer settings, and registry modifications. Administrators can leverage GPP to streamline configuration management tasks and automate common administrative tasks, reducing manual intervention and improving efficiency.

Implementing Group Policy Central Store: The Group Policy Central Store is a centralized repository for Group Policy Administrative Templates (ADMX/ADML files), which define the available policy settings and their descriptions. By creating a Central Store, administrators ensure consistency and standardization across Group Policy settings, regardless of the management workstation used to edit policies.

Leveraging Group Policy Preferences for Software Deployment: Group Policy Preferences can be used to deploy software applications to user or computer targets based on predefined conditions. Administrators can configure software deployment settings such as installation behavior, application removal, and targeting criteria using Group Policy Preferences, simplifying software management tasks and ensuring compliance with organizational standards.

Optimizing Group Policy Performance: Advanced Group Policy management includes techniques for optimizing Group Policy processing performance to minimize delays and improve overall system responsiveness. Strategies for optimizing Group Policy performance include reducing the number of GPOs, disabling unnecessary settings, enabling client-side caching, and implementing loopback processing where appropriate.

Automating Group Policy Management Tasks: Automation tools such as PowerShell can be used to automate common Group Policy management tasks such as creating, modifying, and linking GPOs, configuring security filtering, and applying

Group Policy settings. By automating repetitive tasks, administrators can streamline Group Policy management and ensure consistency across the network environment.

Auditing and Monitoring Group Policy Changes: Auditing and monitoring Group Policy changes are essential for maintaining security and compliance in Active Directory environments. Administrators can use tools like Advanced Group Policy Management (AGPM) or third-party auditing solutions to track changes to Group Policy objects, review policy settings, and detect unauthorized modifications.

Advanced Group Policy management strategies empower administrators to achieve greater control, flexibility, and efficiency in managing their network environments. By mastering advanced techniques such as filtering, item-level targeting, and automation, administrators can streamline configuration management, enhance security, and optimize the performance of their Active Directory infrastructure.

In summary, this chapter has explored advanced Group Policy management strategies that enable administrators to leverage the full potential of Group Policy for efficient configuration management in Active Directory environments. By implementing these strategies and best practices, administrators can optimize Group Policy management, improve system performance, and enhance security across their network infrastructure.

Chapter 8: Active Directory Database Maintenance and Optimization

Database defragmentation and compaction are essential maintenance tasks for ensuring the optimal performance and efficiency of databases in various systems, including Active Directory environments. This chapter explores advanced strategies for managing database fragmentation and compaction, focusing on techniques to identify fragmentation, tools to perform defragmentation and compaction, and best practices for maintaining database health.

Understanding Database Fragmentation: Database fragmentation refers to the phenomenon where data becomes scattered across the storage space, leading to inefficient data retrieval and storage operations. Fragmentation can occur due to frequent data modifications, such as inserts, updates, and deletes, which result in the storage of data in non-contiguous blocks.

Identifying Fragmentation in Active Directory Databases: To identify fragmentation in Active Directory databases, administrators can use the Performance Monitor tool (Perfmon) to monitor performance counters related to database performance metrics such as disk I/O, disk latency, and database read/write operations.

bashCopy code

```
perfmon
```

Perfmon provides real-time performance monitoring capabilities, allowing administrators to analyze database performance metrics and identify signs of fragmentation.

Analyzing Database Fragmentation Levels: Tools like the Active Directory Database Maintenance (NTDSUtil) command-line tool can be used to analyze fragmentation levels in Active Directory databases. The Files subcommand in NTDSUtil provides options to examine database integrity and fragmentation.

bashCopy code

```
ntdsutil "Files" "Info"
```

Running this command in NTDSUtil provides information about the size and fragmentation level of the Active Directory database files.

Performing Database Defragmentation: Active Directory databases can be defragmented using the Optimize subcommand in NTDSUtil. This command compacts the database files and reclaims unused space, improving database performance and reducing fragmentation.

bashCopy code

```
ntdsutil "Files" "Optimize"
```

Executing this command initiates the database optimization process, which defragments and compacts the Active Directory database files.

Scheduling Regular Maintenance Tasks: To maintain database health and prevent fragmentation, administrators should schedule regular maintenance tasks, including database defragmentation and compaction. These tasks can be automated using scheduled tasks or PowerShell scripts to ensure consistent performance optimization.

Monitoring Database Growth and Usage Patterns: Monitoring database growth and usage patterns is essential for identifying potential fragmentation issues proactively. Administrators can use tools like Performance

Monitor and PowerShell scripts to track database growth rates, disk usage, and performance metrics over time.

Implementing Disk Defragmentation: In addition to database defragmentation, administrators should also perform disk defragmentation on the storage volumes hosting Active Directory database files. Disk defragmentation helps optimize disk storage and improves overall system performance by organizing data in contiguous blocks.

bashCopy code

```
defrag C: /X
```

This command initiates the disk defragmentation process for the specified drive (in this case, drive C:) and displays detailed progress information.

Monitoring Performance After Defragmentation: After performing database defragmentation and disk defragmentation, administrators should monitor system performance to ensure that fragmentation levels have been reduced and performance has improved. Performance monitoring tools like Perfmon can be used to track database performance metrics and assess the impact of defragmentation.

Documenting Maintenance Procedures: It is essential to document database maintenance procedures, including defragmentation and compaction tasks, to ensure consistency and repeatability. Documentation should include details such as the frequency of maintenance tasks, the tools and commands used, and any specific considerations for the environment.

Database defragmentation and compaction are critical maintenance tasks for ensuring the optimal performance and efficiency of Active Directory databases. By understanding fragmentation, using appropriate tools and commands, and following best practices for maintenance, administrators can mitigate fragmentation issues and maintain database health in Active Directory environments.

In summary, this chapter has explored advanced strategies for managing database fragmentation and compaction in Active Directory environments. By implementing proactive maintenance practices, monitoring database performance, and leveraging appropriate tools and commands, administrators can optimize database performance and ensure the reliability and efficiency of Active Directory services.

Implementing database integrity checks is a crucial aspect of maintaining the health and reliability of databases in any system, including Active Directory environments. This chapter explores the importance of database integrity checks, various techniques for performing these checks, and best practices for ensuring data consistency and reliability.

Understanding Database Integrity: Database integrity refers to the accuracy, consistency, and reliability of data stored within a database. It ensures that data meets predefined constraints, such as referential integrity, data types, and uniqueness, to maintain data reliability and prevent corruption.

Importance of Database Integrity Checks: Database integrity checks are essential for detecting and preventing data corruption, ensuring data consistency, and maintaining database reliability. By regularly performing integrity checks, administrators can identify and resolve issues early, minimizing the risk of data loss or corruption.

Types of Database Integrity Checks: There are several types of integrity checks that can be performed on databases, including:

Physical Integrity Checks: These checks verify the physical structure of the database files to ensure that they are not corrupt or damaged.

Logical Integrity Checks: These checks verify the logical consistency of the data stored within the database, such as ensuring referential integrity constraints are met.

Data Integrity Checks: These checks verify the accuracy and completeness of the data stored within the database, such as checking for duplicate records or missing data.

Performing Physical Integrity Checks: Tools like the **ntdsutil** command-line utility in Active Directory can be used to perform physical integrity checks on the Active Directory database files.

bashCopy code

```
ntdsutil "Files" "Integrity"
```

Running this command in **ntdsutil** initiates a physical integrity check on the Active Directory database files to ensure they are structurally sound and not corrupt.

Performing Logical Integrity Checks: Logical integrity checks can be performed using tools like the **dcdiag** command-line utility in Active Directory, which checks for logical consistency issues within the Active Directory database.

bashCopy code

```
dcdiag /test:checksecurityerror /v
```

This command executes the **checksecurityerror** test in **dcdiag** to verify the integrity of security descriptors in Active Directory objects.

Performing Data Integrity Checks: Data integrity checks can be performed using SQL queries or PowerShell scripts to validate the accuracy and completeness of data stored within the database. For example, administrators can use SQL queries to identify duplicate records or missing data in specific tables.

sqlCopy code

```
SELECT * FROM TableName GROUP BY ColumnName HAVING COUNT(*) > 1
```

This SQL query identifies duplicate records in the specified table based on the values in the specified column.

Automating Integrity Checks: To ensure regular and consistent integrity checks, administrators can automate the process using scheduled tasks or PowerShell scripts. These scripts can be configured to run at predefined intervals to perform integrity checks and generate reports on the results.

Interpreting Integrity Check Results: After performing integrity checks, administrators should analyze the results to identify any issues or anomalies. It is essential to understand the significance of each type of integrity check and take appropriate action based on the results.

Implementing Remediation Strategies: If integrity checks uncover any issues or inconsistencies, administrators should implement remediation strategies to resolve them promptly. This may involve repairing corrupt database files, fixing logical consistency issues, or correcting data errors.

Documenting Integrity Check Procedures: It is essential to document integrity check procedures, including the tools and commands used, the frequency of checks, and any specific considerations for the environment. Documentation helps ensure consistency and provides a reference for troubleshooting and auditing purposes.

In summary, implementing database integrity checks is critical for maintaining the health and reliability of databases in Active Directory environments. By performing regular physical, logical, and data integrity checks, automating the process where possible, and interpreting the results effectively, administrators can identify and resolve issues early, ensuring the integrity and consistency of data stored within the database.

Horizontal and vertical scaling are two fundamental strategies used in scaling computer systems to accommodate increased workload demands. Next, we will explore these strategies, their differences, and the techniques used to implement them effectively.

Understanding Horizontal Scaling: Horizontal scaling, also known as scaling out, involves adding more machines or instances to distribute the workload across multiple servers. This approach increases the capacity of the system by adding more resources in parallel.

Understanding Vertical Scaling: Vertical scaling, also known as scaling up, involves increasing the capacity of existing servers by adding more resources, such as CPU, memory, or storage, to handle increased workload demands. This approach enhances the performance of individual servers.

Key Differences between Horizontal and Vertical Scaling:

Scalability: Horizontal scaling offers better scalability as it can accommodate an unlimited number of servers, while vertical scaling has limitations based on the maximum capacity of individual servers.

Cost: Horizontal scaling can be more cost-effective as it utilizes commodity hardware and allows for incremental additions, whereas vertical scaling may require expensive upgrades to existing hardware.

Complexity: Vertical scaling is simpler to implement as it involves upgrading existing servers, while horizontal scaling requires additional configuration and management of multiple servers.

Common Techniques for Horizontal Scaling:

Load Balancing: Distributing incoming requests across multiple servers using a load balancer ensures even distribution of workload and improves fault tolerance.

Clustering: Creating clusters of servers allows for seamless scaling by adding or removing nodes dynamically based on workload requirements.

Database Sharding: Partitioning databases into smaller, more manageable segments, or shards, distributed across multiple servers improves performance and scalability.

Common Techniques for Vertical Scaling:

Adding Resources: Increasing CPU, memory, or storage capacity of existing servers improves performance and allows them to handle larger workloads.

Hardware Upgrades: Upgrading hardware components such as processors, memory modules, or storage drives enhances server performance and capacity.

Virtualization: Using virtualization technologies allows for better utilization of hardware resources by running multiple virtual machines on a single physical server.

Determining Scalability Requirements: Before choosing between horizontal and vertical scaling, it is essential to assess the scalability requirements of the system, including anticipated workload growth, budget constraints, and performance expectations.

Implementing Horizontal Scaling:

Deploying Load Balancers: Utilizing load balancers such as NGINX or HAProxy to distribute incoming traffic across multiple servers.

Configuring Auto-Scaling Groups: Setting up auto-scaling groups in cloud environments like AWS or Azure to automatically add or remove instances based on predefined metrics.

Utilizing Containerization: Containerization platforms like Docker or Kubernetes facilitate the deployment and management of containerized applications across multiple servers.

Implementing Vertical Scaling:

Upgrading Hardware: Adding more CPU cores, increasing RAM capacity, or installing faster storage drives to existing servers.

Using Virtualization: Leveraging hypervisor technologies such as VMware or Hyper-V to allocate more resources to virtual machines as needed.

Optimizing Configuration: Fine-tuning server configurations, such as adjusting kernel parameters or optimizing database settings, to improve performance.

Combining Horizontal and Vertical Scaling: In some cases, a combination of horizontal and vertical scaling may be necessary to achieve optimal scalability and performance. For example, deploying load balancers to distribute traffic across multiple clusters of vertically scaled servers.

Monitoring and Optimization: Regardless of the scaling strategy employed, continuous monitoring of system performance and workload trends is essential. Monitoring tools like Prometheus or Grafana can provide insights into resource utilization and help identify bottlenecks for optimization.

In summary, horizontal and vertical scaling are two essential strategies for accommodating increased workload demands in computer systems. By understanding the differences between these approaches and implementing appropriate techniques, organizations can achieve scalability, performance, and reliability in their infrastructure deployments.

Designing an Active Directory (AD) infrastructure for scalability is essential for organizations to ensure that their directory service can effectively accommodate growth and handle increased workload demands. Next, we will explore various considerations and best practices for designing a scalable AD infrastructure.

Understanding Scalability Requirements: Before designing an AD infrastructure, it is crucial to assess the organization's scalability requirements. This includes considering factors such as the number of users, devices, applications, and anticipated growth over time.

Choosing the Right AD Forest Topology: The forest topology defines the logical structure of the AD environment and plays a significant role in scalability. Organizations can choose from single forest, multiple forests, or resource forests based on their requirements. For example, a single forest topology simplifies management but may not be suitable for large or geographically dispersed organizations.

Planning Domain Controllers Placement: Proper placement of domain controllers (DCs) is critical for ensuring scalability and fault tolerance. DCs should be strategically distributed across physical locations to minimize latency and provide redundancy. The use of sites and site links in AD Sites and Services helps optimize DC placement.

Scaling Out Domain Controllers: Scaling out domain controllers involves deploying additional DCs to distribute the authentication and directory lookup workload. CLI commands such as dcpromo in Windows Server can be used to promote a server to a domain controller.

Example:

bashCopy code

dcpromo /unattend

Optimizing Replication: AD replication is essential for ensuring data consistency across DCs. Optimizing replication topology and interval settings helps minimize replication latency and ensures timely propagation of changes. Commands like repadmin can be used to monitor and troubleshoot replication.

Example:

bashCopy code

repadmin /showrepl

Implementing Global Catalog Servers: Global Catalog (GC) servers store a partial replica of all objects in the forest and facilitate searching and authentication processes. Deploying GC servers strategically in each site improves query performance and fault tolerance.

Scaling Out DNS Infrastructure: DNS plays a critical role in AD infrastructure for name resolution. Scaling out DNS servers and ensuring DNS redundancy is essential for scalability. Commands like dnscmd can be used to manage DNS servers.

Example:

Copy code

dnscmd /ZoneAdd

Deploying Read-Only Domain Controllers (RODCs): RODCs are ideal for branch office scenarios where physical security cannot be guaranteed. Deploying RODCs helps improve security and scalability by reducing the replication traffic to and from hub sites.

Utilizing Virtualization: Virtualization technologies such as Hyper-V or VMware allow organizations to scale their AD infrastructure more efficiently by dynamically allocating resources to virtual domain controllers based on demand.

Monitoring and Capacity Planning: Continuous monitoring of AD infrastructure performance and capacity planning are essential for identifying scalability bottlenecks and proactively addressing them. Tools like PerfMon and Active Directory Administrative Center provide insights into AD performance metrics.

Disaster Recovery and High Availability: Designing for scalability should also consider disaster recovery and high availability requirements. Implementing solutions such as AD site resilience and backup and restore strategies ensures business continuity in case of failures.

Testing and Validation: Before deploying changes to the AD infrastructure, it is crucial to test and validate the scalability design in a controlled environment. This helps identify potential issues and fine-tune the design before production deployment.

In summary, designing an AD infrastructure for scalability requires careful planning, consideration of various factors, and adherence to best practices. By implementing the right topology, optimizing replication, strategically placing domain controllers, and leveraging virtualization, organizations can build a scalable and robust AD environment to meet their evolving needs.

Chapter 10: Disaster Recovery Planning and Testing

Developing Active Directory (AD) disaster recovery plans is critical for ensuring business continuity and minimizing downtime in the event of unexpected incidents. This chapter will explore the key considerations, strategies, and best practices for developing effective AD disaster recovery plans.

Understanding Disaster Recovery Requirements: Before developing a disaster recovery plan, it is essential to understand the organization's requirements, including recovery time objectives (RTOs) and recovery point objectives (RPOs). This involves assessing the criticality of AD services, applications, and data, as well as regulatory compliance requirements.

Backup and Restore Strategies: Implementing robust backup and restore strategies is fundamental to AD disaster recovery. Regularly backing up AD data, including system state, configuration, and domain partition, ensures that critical information is preserved and can be restored in case of data loss or corruption.

Commands such as wbadmin in Windows Server can be used to perform system state backups.

Example:

```
phpCopy code
wbadmin        start        systemstatebackup        -
backuptarget:<TargetDrive>
```

Selecting Backup Solutions: Choose backup solutions that align with the organization's requirements and budget. Consider factors such as scalability, ease of use, support for granular recovery, and integration with other disaster recovery tools.

Testing Backup and Restore Procedures: Regularly test backup and restore procedures to validate their effectiveness and identify any potential issues or gaps. Conducting scheduled test restores ensures that backups are reliable and can be restored within the required timeframe.

Implementing Redundancy and High Availability: Deploying redundant AD components, such as domain controllers and DNS servers, across multiple sites enhances fault tolerance and reduces the risk of service disruptions. Utilize technologies like AD site resilience, DNS round-robin, and network load balancing (NLB) to achieve high availability.

Documenting Disaster Recovery Procedures: Document detailed disaster recovery procedures, including step-by-step instructions for restoring AD services and data. Ensure that documentation is up-to-date, accessible to relevant stakeholders, and includes contact information for support personnel and vendors.

Establishing Communication Protocols: Define communication protocols and escalation procedures for notifying key stakeholders, such as IT staff, management, and external vendors, in the event of a disaster. Maintain contact lists and ensure that communication channels are accessible and reliable.

Implementing Off-Site Backup Storage: Store backup copies of AD data in secure off-site locations to mitigate the risk of data loss due to on-premises disasters, such as fires, floods, or physical theft. Cloud-based backup solutions offer scalable and cost-effective off-site storage options.

Creating Recovery Plans for Different Scenarios: Develop recovery plans for various disaster scenarios, including hardware failures, data corruption, cyberattacks, and natural disasters. Tailor recovery plans to address specific risks and prioritize critical services and applications for rapid restoration.

Monitoring and Auditing: Implement monitoring and auditing mechanisms to track backup and restore activities, identify potential issues, and ensure compliance with disaster recovery policies and procedures. Use tools like Windows Event Viewer and AD replication monitoring tools to monitor AD health and performance.

Training and Awareness Programs: Conduct regular training sessions and awareness programs for IT staff and other stakeholders to familiarize them with disaster recovery procedures, roles, and responsibilities. Provide hands-on training and simulations to ensure readiness during actual emergencies.

Continuous Improvement and Review: Continuously review and update disaster recovery plans to incorporate lessons learned from past incidents, changes in technology, and evolving business requirements. Conduct periodic reviews and audits to validate the effectiveness of the disaster recovery strategy.

In summary, developing effective Active Directory disaster recovery plans requires thorough planning, testing, documentation, and collaboration across the organization. By implementing robust backup and restore strategies, establishing redundancy and high availability, documenting recovery procedures, and conducting regular training and testing, organizations can mitigate the impact of disasters and ensure the resilience of their AD infrastructure.

Conducting disaster recovery drills and testing is an essential aspect of maintaining the resilience and effectiveness of disaster recovery plans. This chapter will explore the importance of disaster recovery drills, the different types of testing methodologies, and best practices for conducting successful drills.

Importance of Disaster Recovery Drills: Disaster recovery drills simulate real-world scenarios and allow organizations to validate the effectiveness of their recovery plans, identify gaps or weaknesses, and train personnel on their roles and responsibilities during emergencies. Drills also help build confidence among stakeholders and ensure readiness to respond to unforeseen events.

Types of Testing Methodologies: There are several testing methodologies that organizations can use to evaluate their disaster recovery plans:

a. **Tabletop Exercises**: Tabletop exercises involve scenario-based discussions and decision-making exercises conducted in a simulated environment. Participants discuss how they would respond to different disaster scenarios and identify areas for improvement.

b. **Structured Walkthroughs**: Structured walkthroughs involve step-by-step reviews of the disaster recovery plan, focusing on each phase of the recovery process. Participants examine the plan's documentation, procedures, and communication protocols to identify potential issues or gaps.

c. **Partial Failover Testing**: Partial failover testing involves selectively failing over specific components or services to alternate infrastructure or data centers. This allows organizations to assess the impact of partial failures on critical systems and validate the failover mechanisms.

d. **Full-Scale Simulation**: Full-scale simulation tests replicate real-world disaster scenarios as closely as possible, including the activation of backup systems, restoration of data, and coordination of response activities. These tests provide the most comprehensive evaluation of the disaster recovery plan's effectiveness.

Planning and Preparation: Before conducting a disaster recovery drill, organizations should carefully plan and prepare for the exercise. This includes defining clear objectives, selecting appropriate scenarios, identifying participants and their roles, scheduling the drill, and securing necessary resources and facilities.

Scenario Development: Develop realistic disaster scenarios that align with potential threats and risks faced by the organization. Scenarios should cover a range of events, such as natural disasters, cyberattacks, hardware failures, and human errors. Tailor scenarios to test specific aspects of the recovery plan, such as data restoration, communication procedures, and decision-making processes.

Execution and Evaluation: During the drill, participants follow the predefined procedures outlined in the disaster recovery plan to respond to the simulated disaster scenario. Facilitators observe the drill, document observations and feedback, and assess the effectiveness of the response. After the drill, conduct a thorough debriefing session to review lessons learned, identify areas for improvement, and document action items.

Iterative Improvement: Use the insights gained from disaster recovery drills to iteratively improve the disaster recovery plan. Update documentation, revise procedures, and implement corrective actions to address identified weaknesses or deficiencies. Regularly schedule follow-up drills and testing to validate improvements and maintain readiness.

Documentation and Reporting: Document the outcomes of disaster recovery drills, including observations, findings, and recommendations for improvement. Prepare a comprehensive report summarizing the drill's objectives, scenarios, participant feedback, and lessons learned. Share the report with key stakeholders and management to drive accountability and support ongoing improvements.

Integration with Change Management: Integrate disaster recovery testing into the organization's change management processes to ensure that updates or changes to IT systems and infrastructure are properly tested and validated. Coordinate with IT operations teams to schedule testing windows and minimize disruption to production environments.

Training and Awareness: Provide regular training and awareness programs to educate employees about disaster recovery procedures, roles, and responsibilities. Ensure that personnel are familiar with the steps they need to take during emergencies and understand how their actions contribute to the organization's overall resilience.

Regulatory Compliance and Reporting: Ensure that disaster recovery drills comply with regulatory requirements and industry standards. Maintain documentation of drill activities and outcomes to demonstrate compliance during audits or regulatory inspections. Use compliance frameworks such as NIST SP 800-34 to guide disaster recovery planning and testing efforts.

In summary, conducting disaster recovery drills and testing is essential for validating the effectiveness of disaster recovery plans, identifying areas for improvement, and building organizational resilience. By following best practices for planning, scenario development, execution, and evaluation, organizations can ensure that they are well-prepared to respond to and recover from unexpected events.

Conclusion

In this comprehensive book bundle, we have delved deep into the world of Active Directory and network management, providing essential knowledge and advanced techniques for system administrators and IT security professionals alike. Across four books, we have covered everything from the fundamentals of Active Directory management to advanced techniques for optimization and troubleshooting.

Book 1, "Active Directory Essentials: A Beginner's Guide to Windows Network Management," serves as the perfect introduction for those new to Active Directory. It covers the foundational concepts and basic operations necessary for effective network management in a Windows environment.

Book 2, "Mastering Active Directory: Advanced Techniques for System Administrators," takes readers on a journey into the more intricate aspects of Active Directory management. From group policy implementation to multi-domain architectures, this book equips administrators with the knowledge and skills needed to manage complex network infrastructures.

Book 3, "Securing Active Directory: Strategies and Best Practices for IT Security Professionals," addresses the critical importance of securing Active Directory against various cyber threats. With in-depth discussions on authentication mechanisms, access control, and audit policies, this book empowers security professionals to safeguard their organization's most valuable assets.

Book 4, "Active Directory Troubleshooting and Optimization: Expert Tips for Peak Performance and Resilience," provides invaluable insights into diagnosing and resolving common issues that may arise in Active Directory environments. From replication problems to performance bottlenecks, this book offers expert guidance for maintaining optimal functionality and resilience.

Together, these four books form a comprehensive guide to Active Directory and network management, covering everything from the basics to advanced techniques and best practices. Whether you're a beginner seeking to establish a solid foundation or an experienced professional looking to fine-tune your skills, this book bundle has something for everyone. With the knowledge gained from these books, system administrators and IT security professionals can confidently manage and secure their Active Directory environments, ensuring the reliability and integrity of their organization's network infrastructure.